When Life Blows You Down

11 ½ WAYS TO GET UP AND THRIVE
WHEN THE WINDS OF CHANGE HOWL

BILL DYER

Quantum Leap Resources
Jacksonville, Florida

Published by:
Quantum Leap Resources
7660 Smullian Trail West
Jacksonville, FL 32217

ISBN: 0-9727817-0-6
LCCN: 2003090826

PERMISSIONS:
I would like to acknowledge the following publishers for permission to reprint the following material:

"The Invitation" from THE INVITATION by ORIAH MOUNTAIN DREAMER. Copyright © 1999 by Oriah Mountain Dreamer. Reprinted by permission of Harper Collins Publishers Inc.

Excerpt from THE GREATEST MIRACLE IN THE WORLD by Og Mandino, copyright. Used by permission of Bantam Books, a division of Random House, Inc.

DISCLAIMER:
The purpose of this book is to educate and inspire. It is sold with the understanding that the publisher and author are not engaged in rendering counseling and therapy. If such assistance is required by the reader - the services of a competent professional should be sought.

The author and the publisher, Quantum Leap Resources, shall have neither liability nor responsibility to any person or entity with respect to any loss or damage caused, or alleged to have been caused, directly or indirectly, by the information and message contained in this book. If you do not wish to be bound by the above, you may return this book to the publisher for a full refund.

Cover design by Dunn & Associates Design
Back cover writing by Susan Kendrick Writing
Interior book design by Janice M. Phelps

PRINTED IN THE UNITED STATES OF AMERICA

Dedicated to my mother and father

"Love is the persistent effort of one person to create for another,
The environment in which the other,
Can become the man or woman he or she was meant to be."
– Unknown

Ma and Pa, *thank you* for loving me that way.
This book is a product of your love.

TABLE OF CONTENTS

Acknowledgments

I wish to take a moment and give thanks to those who contributed to this endeavor.

To my friends Margot Robinson and Jim Folks: To Jim, for your invitation to meet at your place for breakfast and my first writing lesson — during which time I saw myself as an author for the first time and was inspired to begin writing every day. To Margot, for helping me organize my thoughts and create an outline that made this book real to me, long before it was real to anyone else.

To my friends everywhere who supported and encouraged me along the journey of creating this book. I made a list to include here and each time I thought it was complete, another person came to mind. At last, I have decided to express my thanks in this all-inclusive way so that I prevent missing someone special. One thing I am sure about is how fortunate I am to have so many kind, caring, extraordinary people in my life. Each of you believed in me, and in your own wonderful and unique way, helped keep my dreams alive and real.

My special thanks to all the supportive and enthusiastic people who took the time to review the manuscript and provide feedback, including the following people for doing such a thorough job and being so honest, bold, and straight with your feedback. To my mom and dad, Ann and Jim Dyer and the rest of my immediate family — Hayden and Phil Behnke, Greg and Mary Beth Dyer, and Brad and Gail Johnson. Thanks also to Dr. Vernon Sylvest, Lisa Watson, Matt Graham, Kim Chappell, and Jean Pope. This book reflects the input you gave to specifically enhance the value to the reader. It is a better book because of your generosity and I am greatly appreciative.

Writing certain portions of this book would not have been possible without the awareness I have gained from many workshops, seminars, books, and tapes. Thanks to all the authors, facilitators, presenters, and coaches who deepened my understanding of why we operate the way we do as human beings, and how we can remove the obstacles that keep us from reaching our full potential. Thanks especially to the growth made possible by the following organizations: Destiny Seminars, The Kairos Foundation, Landmark Education, The Pacific Institute, and Stop at Nothing.

Last but certainly not least, thanks a million to Janice Phelps for your wonderful talent and insights as an editor. I thoroughly enjoyed working with you and experiencing the positive energy you brought to this project. I look forward to the next time.

A portion of the proceeds from the sale of this book will support charities that help people who have been impacted by crime, domestic violence, or homelessness.

In a "New York Minute" Everything Can Change

YOU WAKE UP ON A BEAUTIFUL MORNING, BUT IT IS HARD TO ENJOY the day. Life hasn't gone well lately. Something challenging has happened, and it's not good for you or someone you love. You wish the circumstances could be different. You've experienced happier times, when you weren't dealing with this present situation. If only you could snap your fingers and make all the unpleasant stuff go away. To some degree, you've had a Lifeblow.

Regardless of their nature or size, a LIFEBLOW is any unplanned, unexpected, or uninvited change event that leaves you angry or upset to any degree.

As human beings, our lives can be hit by howling winds of change; irritating, maddening, and saddening events that try our patience, ruin our day, and upset our routine. Some blows in life are bigger. They blow you down, trample your spirit, break your heart, level your hope, and leave you questioning yourself and your resolve. Regardless of the size of your Lifeblows and whether they affect you for a day, a year, or a lifetime — this book provides a formula for being your best during difficult times and awakening each day with a reason to smile.

THERE ARE MANY SCENARIOS FOR LIFEBLOWS:

- getting a flat tire on the way to an important appointment,
- having your car break down in the middle of nowhere,
- running out of gas on a busy highway,
- missing a deadline,
- your computer crashing and losing hours of time and work,
- being involved in a car wreck,
- being the victim of a crime,
- having a fire at your house,
- waking up to find your apartment flooded,
- getting a speeding ticket,
- having your car damaged in a hailstorm,
- suffering a sporting injury,
- getting cut off in traffic or being tailgated,
- your office calling you while you're on vacation,
- telemarketers calling during dinner,
- getting horrible service or food at a restaurant,
- having a baby and not having a clue about how you'll provide for him/her,
- leaving your organizer on the roof of your car and driving away,
- an airline losing your luggage,
- pipes in your house freezing or bursting;
- slipping on a sidewalk and bruising your backside,
- buying a product that has been misrepresented,
- financial difficulties,

- not being able to pay your bills,
- having to declare bankruptcy,
- struggling in a business venture,
- a business failure,
- starting a business
- losing a major account,
- being told to accept more responsibility at work with no compensation, for the third time,
- adjusting to an organizational change,
- not getting a promotion,
- being fired, laid off, demoted, or getting a bad review from your boss,
- health problems or watching a loved one suffer from a disease or sickness,
- losing an important game or botching a competition after hours, perhaps even years, of preparation,
- the loss of a loved one or pain from seeing your child get hurt or in trouble,
- a divorce or separation or splitting up with your boyfriend or girlfriend,
- being stood up on a date,
- finding out your significant other has been unfaithful,
- having a falling out with someone else — a coworker, customer, associate, friend, child, parent, or other relative,
- moving to a new location and struggling to adjust.
- being injured in an accident

The challenges I've had in my life have been varied in their size and impact, but one in particular is the basis of this book. My biggest Lifeblow occurred on the morning of September 28, 1988, in Rochester, New York. At that time, I was selling commercial explosives to the mining and construction industries and doing quite a bit of traveling. I prepared for work; on that particular day, I had some appointments out of town with plans to entertain clients later in the evening. While eating a bagel and reviewing my day, I had no idea that within the next half hour, I would be struggling for my life and wondering if I would live to see the next day.

While driving out of town that morning before sunrise, I decided to stop at a neighborhood automatic teller machine. It was located just around the corner from where I lived, along a quaint little street lined with various gift stores, sandwich shops, and restaurants I frequented. Although I had sixty dollars in my wallet, I knew I was going to need more cash by the end of the day. After reaching the ATM, I pulled up to the curb, jumped out of my car, walked up to the transaction window, inserted my card, and immediately heard someone behind me. My first thoughts were that a fellow bank customer was approaching from behind, so I turned around to say good morning. The sound of those words never left my lips because, before I could speak, I saw a gun pointed at me.

My heart sank. While the gunman ordered me to get him money, I experienced the sickening feeling that comes with the realization that someone is placing a monetary value on human life, and they had mine in their hands.

I had never had such a feeling in my life. That robbery began the most terrifying experience I have ever had, because shortly thereafter, a gunshot broke the early morning silence. My leg snapped, sending me crashing to the pavement. After I hit the ground, the robber ran away. I immediately tried to stand up. No way. I looked at my leg and it was bent at a weird angle. Disbelief was my first feeling, and I believed I would wake up from this nightmare at any moment. Soon, reality set in; there was a real and very horrifying possibility that I might die, this day, in this street.

Images of my family and friends flashed through my mind. I saw the faces of each significant person in my life. Perhaps I was bringing their image close, so I could at least say goodbye. I started yelling for help, over and over, as loudly and clearly as possible. My hopes rose when I looked down the street and saw headlights of a car approaching. Immediately, I thought to myself, *Thank goodness. This is the help I desperately need.*

As the car approached, I raised myself up on my elbow to wave and make sure they saw me so they could stop to help. My hope continued to build as the car slowly approached and got closer and closer. Suddenly, it swerved to avoid hitting me and kept going. I couldn't believe it! With the tail lights moving away, my hopes were dashed and now my thoughts raced. *I can't believe they didn't stop! No one is going to help me. The robber might come back here and finish me off.* Once again, I slipped back to the place in my mind where I could see the faces of people I loved. If I was going to die, I wanted to take those images with me. Suddenly, I snapped out of my trance and was filled with anger. *Not me. I'm not going to die like this in the street. Not if I have anything to say about it.*

I immediately began strategizing. If the robber returned to "finish me," being in a shadow up on the sidewalk might save me. If he did return, maybe he wouldn't see me. That began a snail's-paced crawl toward the curb, pausing after each bit of progress to send out a few more calls for help into the darkness.

By the time I reached the curb, I looked toward the ATM window and saw a man slowly walking toward me. There was enough light for me to know he wasn't the robber. He evidently lived in the neighborhood, heard my calls for help, and called the police and paramedics. Before he reached me, all emergency personnel and equipment were on site. After stretching yellow crime-scene tape around the area, cutting off my pants, and taking pictures of my leg, emergency personnel fitted me with an oxygen mask and loaded me into an ambulance.

I remember the minutes in the ambulance on the way to the hospital and feeling relieved to be safe. After reaching the emergency room, I remember watching a monitor showing dye moving through my leg to detect artery damage. Fortunately, after hearing a nurse say the word "amputation," the anesthetic given to me for surgery consumed me and I lost consciousness. The worst day of my life ended at around 6:00 AM.

When I woke up after my first surgery, I still had my leg, but learned I would be in traction for an undetermined amount of time. I was twenty-seven years old and my entire life was ahead of me. Before now, my biggest challenges related to school, finding a job, moving across the country and to a foreign country to work, but nothing this big or sudden before. Part of me was still thinking that maybe I'd be waking up from a nightmare any minute. You may be able to relate: Sometimes we just don't think some things will happen to us. Confused and shocked, my mind was full of zero understanding, zero hope, and zero peace. I was at my Personal Ground Zero.

I use the term ground zero because in the midst of writing this book, I was driving to the post office on the morning of September 11, 2001. I heard the devastating news of the terrorist attacks where commercial airplanes were used as missiles on the Pentagon and the World Trade Center. I immediately went home and started watching images of the biggest Lifeblow our country has suffered since Pearl Harbor. I sat in horror and disbelief watching those hijacked planes fly into buildings, fireballs shooting out of exploding windows, collapsing skyscrapers, panicked people running for their lives, shocked onlookers who, like most of us, felt as if we were watching a movie.

But no . . . it was real. I saw footage of massive and monstrous grey clouds of pulverized steel and concrete, billowing down streets and overtaking people who were running, screaming, and crying. I heard about the number of people unaccounted for, listened to recordings of cell phone calls made to loved-ones by people who knew they would die. I heard the pained, devastated voices of family members whose loved ones were missing. After watching TV all day and night on September 11, 2001, I seriously considered scratching this manuscript.

The experience that inspired me to write this book seemed very insignificant in comparison. I felt like one of the firemen, or a survivor of the attacks, or a family member of a missing or killed loved one, would one day be a much better and more qualified author of a book like this.

My thinking started shifting, however, throughout the week. With more and more exposure to television, listening to people talk, hearing what they said, and observing what people were doing, I recognized and saw evidence of everything I had just finished writing about. All the keys for "Getting Up When Life Blows You Down," were on display in shining examples of the people of our country in the aftermath of this national tragedy. After six days of news, I began writing again, every bit as enthusiastic as I was when I began seriously writing months before.

What follows in this book, is an account of my struggle to deal with being robbed and shot on September 28, 1988. I will share how my life went into a tailspin during the next few months in the hospital and how my negative thoughts generated feelings and actions that created a miserable existence. I have used my experience to demonstrate how we react to our challenges as human beings and help you understand how we often pay a big price for those automatic human reactions. Using examples from my recovery process, you will see how we can sabotage the areas of life we value most, before we even realize what we are doing. You will see how our reactions to small challenges (like a flat tire) often create more challenges or mini-Lifeblows and how, when enough of those challenges are added together — they can have the same impact as a much bigger Lifeblow event.

I will share the insights, tools, and thought processes that transformed the aftermath of my Lifeblow from miserable to fulfilling. I will explain how life challenges can take on new meaning and how we can bring a new perspective to our day in a way that improves the quality of our life experience. You will have a chance to apply one of your Lifeblows to the same process, and we will consider what people did when the terrorists attacked, that support the points I make for "Getting Up When Life Blows You Down." You might want to keep a journal nearby as you read this book, and thoroughly answer the questions posed throughout, as they are an integral part of the process of working through your Lifeblow.

The purpose of this book is not an attempt to minimize the significance of your challenge or discredit your subsequent thoughts and feelings. The spirit of this book in no way resembles that of the ridiculous question, "Other than that, Mrs. Lincoln, how did the play go?" The spirit of this book is to awaken your inherent ability to rise above life challenges that blow you down to your personal ground zero and give you strength to stand up tall with a smile on your face. The only tool you need to do that is already inside of you. You'll recognize it in yourself after reading the following story of another Lifeblow I had.

While attending college in New Orleans in 1983, I lived with my best friend from high school, Mike Burnett, in a basement apartment. One night, I could hear the rain outside coming down in sheets. Before drifting off to sleep, I remember listening to the sound of rain pounding against my window, accompanied by an occasional burst of thunder and flash of lightening. I felt very happy to be in a dry and comfortable bed.

My next conscious thoughts were the foggy kind after being suddenly awakened from a deep sleep. My bed was shaking and as I woke up, I found myself trying to figure out where in the world I was. It was still dark and as my eyes strained to see something that would explain what was happening, I saw Mike's silhouette standing at the foot of my bed. Then I heard his voice, "Bill, Bill, wake up, wake up!"

"Okay, okay — what's going on?" I replied.

Mike then said the most confusing thing to me, "Can I get on the bed with you?"

Not quite sure I had heard him clearly, I said, "What?"

The reply was the same — "Can I get on the bed with you?" I was fully awake now.

I knew Mike like my brother, so I knew he wasn't suddenly attracted to me in a way I was unaware of before now. We had double dated since high school and had had many conversations trying to figure out the "female species." Even so, I did think his request was very odd, so I didn't just say, "Oh sure," and scoot on over. I had to dig deeper, "What are you saying? What are you doing?"

His answer was the same, "Can I please get on the bed with you?"

Still not understanding any of this, I sat up, shook my groggy head, and asked, "Why Mike? I don't get it."

He said, "Why? You want to know *why*? Put your hand over the side of the bed."

I rolled over, threw my hand over the side of the mattress, and the awakening was rude. I finally understood the strange behavior of my friend, when my hand plunged into cold water. It had rained about twelve inches during the night and we had a foot and a half of water in our apartment. Mike's bed consisted of box springs and a mattress on the floor, so he had already been flooded out of his warm cocoon. Soaking wet, he was now in search of a dry place to sleep. My bed included a frame and was off the floor, high and dry. Mike is no dummy. He wanted a piece of it.

When I understood Mike's situation, I welcomed him onto my "raft." That was a big mistake. There we were, our combined weights totaling over 500 pounds, and it didn't take long for the sagging bed to become a huge sponge. Moments later, the box springs, mattress, sheets, and Bill were as soaked as the big wet rat that had just climbed on. Since it was still dark outside and the electricity was out, there really wasn't anything to do but lie there miserable and wet, cussing under our breath, staring into the darkness in disbelief, and waiting for the sun to come up. I guess we figured that daylight would shed some light on what to do next.

When dawn's first light came through the window, the first thing I noticed was an old milk crate, full of my albums. It was listing in the water, and the sight of it made us wonder: What other possessions of ours were now under water and probably ruined? Suddenly there was much to do: to go on a mission to find and salvage everything that meant something to us. As we waded through the apartment, almost simultaneously Mike and I remembered our dogs, Max and Jet! The entire time we had been awake, we hadn't heard a peep out of either one. Immediately our thoughts and concern for them became intense and frantic.

Jet was a two-month-old Labrador retriever puppy and Max was a ninety-pound Siberian husky/golden retriever mixture. Since Jet was a puppy and still being house-trained, he spent nights in our laundry room so he wouldn't do his business elsewhere during the night. He's the first one we went after. When we opened the laundry room door, there he was, paddling around the small room with his head barely above the water. He had a wide-eyed look of total confusion, which changed to immediate relief once he heard his name and saw the open door and Mike's outstretched hands.

After rescuing Jet, our search turned toward finding Max. He usually slept on the floor at the foot of my bed, and there was no sign of him anywhere. We had already covered most of the apartment, so there weren't many more places to look. He must have heard we were up, but why weren't we finding him and why wasn't he coming to us? I was very worried and started to wonder where and how we would find him. My relief came when I stuck my head in the last place Max could be, the bathroom.

There he was, hunkered down in the only remaining dry place in the entire apartment, the bathtub. When he saw me, his tail thumped a few times against the tub and then stopped. It was a halfhearted wag, as if he was trying to decide if it was really okay to be glad to see me. The water had risen to within an inch from the top of the tub. As Max switched glances between the water and me, he had the same incredulous look I'm sure I did when Mike first requested some space on my bed.

From the moment the dogs were accounted for, we started the process of dealing with our situation. We lifted Max and Jet onto a reinforced ping-pong table and decided to find refuge that day with a friend who lived a few blocks away in a second-floor apartment. Just after pulling the front door closed, but before wading down the street, I looked through the window to make sure the dogs were still okay. Max was lying down on top of the ping-pong table and Jet was crouched down at the edge of it, his rear end straight up in the air, looking like he might be trying to keep himself from falling off. Just as I called his name, his body disappeared over the side. I looked at Mike and said, "Jet just fell in." We both knew we had to go back in and rescue him.

When we opened the door, we both saw a sight that we couldn't help but smile about. Jet hadn't fallen off the table. A duck decoy had floated out of a closet near the kitchen. Jet had never seen a duck before, but obviously, instinctively, he wanted it. He wanted it badly enough, in fact, that he had jumped off the table and was halfway across the living room, swimming like a champion toward his heart's desire!

I think about the Great Flood of '83 from time to time. I can't see or read a news story about flooding, without thinking of our experience, feeling sorry for the victims, and being thankful that we didn't lose much. At that stage in our lives, we didn't have much to lose. To this day, Mike and I periodically laugh about our memories of "the night when the water came."

My experience with the flood in our apartment holds powerful insights for overcoming challenges. When challenging floodwaters rise up in our life, we have three choices:

Choice #1:
We can be like Mike and find a friend to
involve in our misery.

Choice #2:
We can be like Max and retreat to higher ground,
silently hoping our challenge goes away.

Choice #3:
We can be like Jet and, ready or not,
learn how to swim —
and get more of what we want in the process.

This book is about learning how to swim when life's challenging floodwaters rise up in your life. It's a book about how to cause and create more of the life you want, by choice. **It's a book that does NOT attempt to make your challenge fulfilling, but simply provides a guide for what you can do to *create fulfillment*, in the face of your Lifeblow.**

When asked to comment on life, Robert Frost said, "It goes on." He was right. The world does not stop turning. Time may seem to stand still in the aftermath of some Lifeblows, but life does indeed go on. *How* it goes on is the difference between whether life is fulfilling or not. Regardless of how you are handling the challenging floodwaters in your life, the spirit of this book is to help you through an after-Lifeblow process for generating, causing, and creating more fulfillment instead of wishing, hoping, and waiting for life to somehow get better.

PART ONE

After Life Delivers a Blow

CHAPTER 1

Lifeblow Reactions at Personal Ground Zeros

*"If I had just stopped for a minute to think before acting,
my entire life would be different."*
—"Sandman," prison inmate

ALONG LIFE'S JOURNEY, WE ARE ALL MOVING FROM A PLACE CALLED Current Reality, to another point in time. It is safe to say that we would like the "other point in time," to include a better, more fulfilling experience of life. We want and desire an improved life full of wonderful relationships. We value and cherish ourselves and our freedom, safety, health, friends, and the members of our family. We wake up every morning wanting fulfillment in the areas we value, but sometimes something happens. We have a Lifeblow. Some challenging event shatters our routine and throws up a serious obstacle to our happiness.

Before we continue, identify a specific Lifeblow you have had and would like to work through as you read this book. Choose a challenge that has you feeling down in the dumps, miserable, angry, disappointed, discouraged, afraid, frustrated, or wondering if or when things will ever be better. You see few, if any, positive aspects to your challenge. Perhaps you find yourself in an almost continuous complaint about your situation.

It could be a recent Lifeblow or an unpleasant experience from the distant past. It could be a challenge that you are sick and tired of being sick and tired about, or a setback that unfolded yesterday. It could be a formidable challenge that keeps you awake at night or a minor obstacle that bugs you like a gnat wanting to make your ear its new home. It could be a challenge you have faced before, or not.

It could be a personal or professional challenge, a challenge that falls into any of our key life areas:

- health,
- relationships,
- family,
- career,
- spiritual,
- financial, or
- hobbies and favorite pastimes.

Take a moment to identify your Lifeblow before reading further. Perhaps write it on a Post-it note and place it on this page.

Since Lifeblows are often part of this life as a human being, one very interesting question is, "Why are some people able to rise above even life's most mountainous challenges and find fulfillment, joy, and peace, while others are not?" The answer is very simple. The people who get up from their personal ground zero have made a distinction that the people who stay down have not. That distinction pertains to the two ways life can occur to us as human beings. The following quote by Aldous Huxley contains that distinction.

"Experience is not what happens to a man or woman. Experience is what a man or woman, DOES with what happens to them."

This quote indicates that, as a human being, I can experience my life in one of two ways:

My experience of life is based on
WHAT HAPPENS TO ME.
– OR –
My experience of life is based on
WHAT I DO _WITH_ WHAT HAPPENS TO ME.

When our experience of life is based on "what happens to me," we wake up, live our life, and have our experiences, which are followed by our automatic way of thinking, feeling, and acting. It is human nature to wake up in the morning and live our life in such a way. I refer to this way of living as *reactive* thinking and behaving. We don't give any thought to what we think, how we feel, or what we do — we simply *are* that way and *do* whatever we do. There's not a thing wrong with thinking and feeling however we do, but we often overlook how our automatic reactions influence the quality of our life. As human beings, we react to our Lifeblows (big and small) and sometimes create more challenges in the process — taking ourselves further off track from having the life we want. The following scenario provides an example of this.

Imagine that you are on your way home from work. A ton of changes are taking place there. The pressure is on and this particular day has been just terrible. Everything that could have gone wrong went wrong with systems, coworkers, and customers. "Murphy" ruled your day. You are driving home now, full of anger and upset. As you pass a slower car, you look into the rearview mirror and see another car barreling down on you. This guy is all over your bumper, tailgating you in a major way. You have no idea how this car is not hitting you. You glance back at this idiot and he is pumping his fist at you. He's flashing his lights and honking his horn. This is the last straw for you. You become enraged at the recklessness and disrespect being demonstrated behind you.

As human beings, we have many reactions to such incidents. Some of us s–l–o–w down. Some of us let him go by and then get on his tail to give him some of his own medicine. Some of us have a favorite gesture reserved for people like this. We might shake our fist back at him or, while he goes by, give him some sign language that lets him know he's "# 1." Some of us just let him go by; it's just not worth getting involved.

There are a lot of crazy things happening in the world. Road rage stories are all over the news. Let's suppose you are a person who slows down for a while but then lets the guy pass and "fly on." You do that, but even so, this experience has you boiling over by the time you reach home.

Things haven't been going well there lately either and you walk through the door with a scowl on your face. Your significant other sarcastically says, "My my, don't we look chipper this evening."

You slam the door, smash your keys down on the counter, and grumble, "Leave me alone!" Then you storm into another room.

Moments later this most important person in your life walks in behind you and in a raised voice says, "Now wait just a minute! I had a tough day, too. Don't talk to me that way, you jerk!"

Although each of us expresses our frustration and anger in different ways, if you can see yourself, even a tiny bit, in the above scenario, you will notice that your reaction has created a nice little upheaval at home. More unpleasant words are exchanged, followed by some mutual "silent treatment." The energy in your house is as negative as negative gets. Being home isn't any fun either, so you just decide to go to bed early. Putting up with this just isn't in the cards tonight. Granted, you aren't even tired yet, but "playing possum" is so much easier than dealing with the fallout of your Lifeblow. Eventually, there you both are, lying in bed as far away as you can possibly get without touching one another. You eventually fall to sleep, but the upheaval you created doesn't magically disappear over night. You wake up and the house still rumbles with feelings of hurt, anger and resentment. Not much time is wasted getting out of the house and going back in to work.

Once you are at work, someone asks you about that sweet spouse of yours, and you hit the ceiling — leaving them completely confused. They thought you were so pleasant and "in love" at the company picnic a few months ago. The next person you see says, "Good morning," and you mumble something that leaves them looking back at you in disdain. They turn back and walk in the direction they were headed, cussing you under their breath. A short time later, they see another coworker and encourage them to stay away from the monster they just encountered. Word quickly spreads about you, until one person defends you because you had confided to them all that happened to you yesterday. They tell those who criticize your behavior to "mind their own business and 'lay off.' " Now there's an argument fully under way of which you aren't even aware.

You don't realize it, but many people at work are avoiding you today. They're withholding their time, talent, skills, and cooperation. Since you all need one another, you have not only negatively impacted your relationship at home, you've also done so at work. Morale, teamwork, team spirit, group synergy, key payoff activities, performance, and productivity suffer and are the consequence of your reaction. I could go on and on with the scenario, because you do go back home again, hopefully. Do you see what's happening if things keep unfolding like this? Your relationship at home will be at the bottom of the barrel, right along with the bottom line of your company. Since your insurance benefits, bonuses, raises, and 401(k) plan are dependent on that bottom line, you are negatively impacting your wallet or pocket book. That's no good. Talk about stressful! You could have a heart attack. Said another way, you have just success-fully sabotaged your success in life, across the board. That's what Marcus Aurelius meant when he said, "How much more grievous are the consequences of our anger than the acts which arouse it."

Since yesterday, all your little Lifeblows and your living life based on "what happens to me," have created circumstances and more reasons to be upset. Little did you recognize that while you were in mid-stride with your reactions. Another interesting and sad point, is that the guy tailgating you last evening, the idiot who sent you over the edge, was a man who had had a day much worse than yours. He was desperately trying to signal to you, to move out of the way because he was rushing his dying child to the hospital.

Like you, he had a story. Everyone has a story. When we cross paths with one another out in the world, we have no idea where anyone is going or coming from, or how they feel about it. The above scenario demonstrates how our lives continue to unfold with esca-lated, unwanted outcomes due to our reaction to Lifeblows. Our reactions create additional challenges for ourselves, regardless of whether we are at home, work, school, the grocery store, or on vaca-tion. The smaller events and our reaction to them, added together, can have a major negative impact on the quality of our life and the life of others. Smaller Lifeblows often build on one another and collectively have the impact of a major Lifeblow. We start out being tailgated and wind up losing our job, marriage, or both. That's what we might get when living our life based on "what happens to me."

From a bad-hair day to a bad morning at an ATM, "Getting Up When Life Blows You Down" requires that you start looking at your-self in a very constructively criticizing way. A great place to start that awareness process is in noticing your reactive self-talk. All reactive actions originate in reactive self-talk, or the *reactive conversation* in your head. The experts say you talk to yourself at a rate of 500–1000 words per minute. You are having a full-blown conversation with yourself virtually every moment of every day. In other words, there is a little voice in your head. It may be the same voice for you that just said, "What voice is he talking about?" Did you notice you saying that to yourself? If so, <u>that's</u> the voice I'm talking about. You are having a full-blown conversation with yourself all the time. Day in and day out, you talk to yourself; in fact, you are talking to yourself right now!

Pause for a moment. See if you can "hear" yourself talk about the demand I just made that you are talking to yourself. What are you saying to yourself? What thoughts are you having about my yelling at you like I know you better than you know yourself? The reactive voice I'm talking about, the voice I'm saying is in your head all of the time, may be the same voice for you that just said something like, "No, I'm not talking to myself! This guy doesn't know me. Who does this demanding idiot think he is?!"

Self-talk is a lot like breathing. Most of the time, we aren't aware that we do it. However, at any time, in any moment, we can become aware. If you've ever attended a workshop on dealing with stress, you likely were taught to become aware of how you breathe. Short, shallow, and fast breathing that results from being under stress can be noticed and shifted so that you take in nice, long, slow, deep breaths that relax you. Just as our breathing can be consciously regulated, we can do a similar technique with our self-talk.

Think of a time when you were in the physical presence of others, but weren't attentive to the conversation taking place. You were somewhere else in your thoughts and another person got your attention by saying, "Hey! Where are you? What are you thinking about?" In that instant, you have been caught, being caught up in your automatic thoughts.

You answer them, saying, "I was thinking about something else."

They ask "What?" and you begin to tell them. In that instant, you have become consciously aware of the 500–1000 words that are running through your head. Before the other person interrupted your thoughts, they were subconsciously running rampant, right along with your breathing.

By becoming aware of your self-talk after a Lifeblow, you are becoming aware of your reactionary thoughts and can then determine if they serve or hurt you. My reactive thoughts and the *feelings those thoughts generated* about being shot, were as follows:

> *Poor pitiful Bill. Life's not fair. I've been the victim of a random act of violence. What in the world is the world coming to? Who can I trust now? I'm wasting time in this hospital! I'm going to lose my job. I was stupid to be at an ATM at 4:30 in the morning with money in my pocket. What are other people going to think of me? I'm sure they'll think I'm stupid too. Why can't the police catch the robber? They must be incompetent. The robber needs to pay for what he did. I'll hunt the robber down myself and beat him to a pulp. I'll beat him so badly that he will never, ever walk again. I've wasted the last two years of my life at work. This whole experience has just jerked the rug right out from under me. All the progress I was making in building my business has been for naught.*

I felt: angry, afraid, upset, cheated, disappointed, discouraged, distrustful, depressed, helpless, frustrated, stupid, sorry for myself, edgy, irritable, hostile, numb, shocked, outraged, hurt, violated, resentful, and hateful.

As a result of acting on the above thoughts and emotions I had in the hospital, an average day in the life of Bill Dyer was a pretty gloomy existence. Most of the time I wanted to be alone. While alone, I beat myself up, rehashing the morning of September 28, 1988, over and over and over again — thinking about what I could have done, should have done, would have done, but didn't do. I looked at police mug shots and stared out the window, craving the chance to get revenge. I visualized what revenge would look like and what I was going to do to the robber when I got my hands on him. Several times a day, I visualized myself finding the robber and putting him in my car, taking him out into the woods, tying him to a tree and beating his legs with an aluminum baseball bat until I was sure he would never walk again. That's all I wanted. That vision consumed me.

I was so wrapped up in my thoughts and feelings that sometimes I wouldn't see the people who came to visit me in the hospital. Nurses would tell me I had a visitor, a friend who wanted to check on me, and I would tell the nurse to get rid of them by saying I was asleep. I remember my parents visiting me early on during my hospital stay, and I was wallowing in my negativity so much, that I didn't have anything to say to them. I remember sitting for hours in uncomfortable silence — silence so thick with negativity, you could cut it with a knife.

These were my *reactions* to my Lifeblow of being robbed and shot. My experience of life was based on "what happens to me." As I mentioned above, there is absolutely nothing wrong with any of my reactive ways, but there is a distinction to make about how my reactive ways were impacting my life. That can be determined by identifying what I got/gained from my reaction, as well as what I lost/missed while reacting.

One of the biggest *payoffs* for my reactive thoughts, feelings and actions — was that I had a *right* to think, feel and act that way. I had a *right* to be mad and angry and distrustful. I had a *right* to be lying there in the hospital bed with a chip on my shoulder, mad at the world. I was up early on my way to work to make an honest buck, minding my own business, and this punk steals my money, takes my freedom, and turns my life upside down. I had a *right* to be left alone if that's what I wanted. I had a *right* to plan my revenge. I had a *right* to be disappointed in people because they don't stop to help. I had a *right* to be upset with doctors and nurses for the pain I was in. I had a *right* to be feeling victimized and violated. I had a *right* to think every thought, to feel every feeling, and to take every action. My *payoff* for my *reaction* was that I got to feel justified for being this way after what happened.

Although there was a *payoff* for my *reaction*, there was also a huge *cost*. I lost a lot as a result of my reaction. I wasted valuable and precious time. My negativity prevented me from being productive or doing anything constructive. My negativity prevented me from making a positive contribution in any way, shape, or form to anybody or anything. I was too angry, exhausted, and stressed out. My reaction *cost* me my relationship with my family, relationships with friends, time with friends and family, the experience of giving and receiving love, having fun, being happy, and experiencing growth, fulfillment, joy, and peace of mind.

If you had asked me before the robbery and shooting, "What are the most important aspects of your life? What do you value most in your life?," one of the things I would have included in my answer was my relationships with family members and friends. I would have told you that I wanted to spend quality time with and create close, loving, special, meaningful relationships with the important people in my life. Now remember, I'm confined to a hospital bed with friends wanting to visit and my parents sitting three feet away. We have this incredible chance to spend some wonderful, quality, special, meaningful, and loving time with one another, but as a result of the shooting and my reaction to it, I'm so wrapped up in my negativity that I'm not even speaking to them!

I'll go to my grave combining all of the above losses together, knowing that my reactions *cost* me my life. I was alive, I had vital signs and a pulse, but I wasn't *living!* I wasn't living because I was doing *nothing* to further any of the things in my life that I really cherished and valued. My reactions killed every chance of saving myself from myself and kept me trapped in a dark cloud at my personal ground zero.

Unfortunately, this scenario is typical of what we often do when we *react* to our Lifeblow. From a bad marriage to a bad day at work, challenges generate reactions that undermine obtaining the life we want. We lose sight of the impact our reactions have on everyone and everything most important to us. Taking an inventory of how we win and how we lose with our reactions, enables us to clearly determine if our *reaction* is costing us more than we'd like.

With regard to my reaction in the hospital after being shot, what was larger — how I won or how I lost? What was larger — getting to be *right* about being mad and feeling justified to beat the robber with a bat or paying the price of wanting a close relationship with my parents, but sabotaging that relationship instead? The answer is obvious. What I lost because of my reaction is so much larger than what I got/gained from my reaction. Even though my reaction was quite natural and understandable, none of that is the issue here. **The issue has nothing to do with whether our reactions are understandable, but whether our understandable reactions create desired outcomes.**

The following story provides a poignant example of this distinction. In a 1990s incident completely unrelated to the terrorist attacks, investigators heard a recorded cockpit conversation between pilots after recovering a black box from a downed airliner. The two commercial pilots were so focused on a burned-out control panel light that they were unaware the plane was losing altitude. The result was a nose down crash in the Florida Everglades that killed more than one hundred passengers. Their *reaction* to their challenge of having a burned-out control panel was very understandable; however, their understandable reaction never gave them a shot at making a successful emergency landing.

When you and I experience and live our lives based on "what happens to me," we are unable to be anything more than a victim of circumstance — someone who is completely out of control of their destiny. Why? All our life results are completely dictated by our natural reaction to **what happens**! Living that way is being controlled by our circumstances. We are allowing our circumstances to dictate the degree to which we experience happiness and fulfillment.

When your life experience is based on "what happens to me," if you wake up and good things happen during the day, you are happy. If, on the other hand, you wake up and a challenging change-provoking experience hits your world, you are instantly thrown into your automatic reactive routine. You get to be *right* about your thoughts and feelings of upset, anger, frustration, hurt, and discouragement, and then *do* what upset, angry, frustrated, hurt, and discouraged people do. Most people live their life this way, until something good enough happens to get them back "up." Obviously the greatest risk of living this way is if your Lifeblow is bigger than your positive experiences, the experiences you psychologically identify as "good" may never be enough to enable you to recover a sense of fulfillment, stability, and happiness. We have all met people who are still miserable and unable to smile for days, weeks, months, and years since experiencing a major Lifeblow. Whatever life threw their way, was more than they were able to overcome; more than could be offset by their good days.

Since good days are mixed with bad days, a life that is lived based on "what happens to me," becomes, at the very least, an emotional roller coaster. One minute you're *up*, the next minute you're *down*, and the same for the next and the next. It's "up and down" and "up and down" and "down and down" and "up and down" and "up and up and up" and "down and . . ." It's an emotional roller coaster that's going nowhere. Since life's ups and downs are never ending, the upset, misery, and stress never ends either. Having life occur as "what happens to me," is a very stress-filled way to live because we have given away our power to be in control of ourselves.

A University of Michigan study determined a direct correlation between control and happiness and found that as a human being, the more control you have, the happier you are.

Nothing generates more misery and complaining in a human being than being controlled. When Lifeblows cause unhealthy automatic reactions in us that go unchecked, we have become a victim of life. Life has the control because life dictates what we think, feel, do, and create. It's as if we are puppets and life is pulling our strings. We get to be *right* about our reaction, yet we are being controlled by our circumstances. That's why we get into a continuous complaint about our unfulfilling life. **We want control as human beings, but subconsciously give it away to our *reaction*.**

I was having lunch one day with a friend of mine who is a doctor. We were discussing the topic of stress and how stressful it is to live a life where we have no control, or at least *feel* out of control. I asked my friend to give me a one-liner about *stress*, that I could use in a speech entitled "Being a Champion of Change." He knew about my being shot, and after I asked him for his wisdom he didn't hesitate long before saying, "Bill, stress is like a bullet, it will kill you."

Every American and most people around the world are experiencing a tremendous amount of stress as a result of the changing world we live in. Hundreds of thousands of people die every day of stress-related medical complications. As we allow life changes to have power over us, we kill our chances of experiencing fulfillment. If that sounds like a hopeless way to live life, the good news is that we all have another option. Option #2 is to experience your life based on "What I do <u>with</u> what happens to me," While Option #1 asks nothing of you, Option #2 asks much of you.

President Bush referred to Option #2 when, in the aftermath of the terrorist attacks, he said, "Our nation will define our times, not be defined by them." He was declaring that our country would not be eternal victims of the attacks. We would, instead, unite and respond to create a better, stronger America.

We must apply this philosophy to our Lifeblow — that we will define the quality of our life in the aftermath of it, as opposed to being defined by what happened. Option #1 is simply going with (and giving into) our human nature. Option #1 is comfortable and natural ... that's why most people take it.

Option #2 is about *responding* to your Lifeblow versus *reacting* to it, and it is the *only* difference between getting up and staying down when the winds of change howl.

"WHAT I *DO* WITH WHAT HAPPENS TO ME":
- will require more effort,
- will ask you to accept more responsibility,
- will require you to adopt a proactive philosophy, rather than staying in a reactive mode,
- will require you to leave your comfort zone,
- will challenge your truths about your life,
- will require you to develop and use your creativity,
- will require you to drop your most prized possession — your ego.

CHAPTER 2

Noticing Unhealthy Reactions
and Stopping the Madness

"The only victory that counts, is the one over yourself."
– Jesse Owens

*T*WO YEARS AFTER I WAS SHOT, I WAS ALMOST KILLED IN AN EXPLOSION while working at Lake Mattamuskeet, a wildlife refuge in eastern North Carolina. My *reaction* and *response* to the events that unfolded on that day were an important test for me, as far as choosing "what to do <u>with</u> what happens to me."

At Lake Mattamuskeet, we were involved in a project where we were creating lakes by blasting huge craters into the marsh. These lakes would provide more refuge for ducks and geese. Sometimes unable to get vehicles near these shots, we often shot without cover, without the benefit of having a large object, such as a truck, to hide behind or crawl underneath if we had to avoid being hit by stumps and logs that were part of the explosion. To make up for this lack of cover, we blasted these craters from a safe distance of several hundred feet. All of these blasts created violent explosions that sent massive amounts of debris into the sky. As the lead man on the job, I continuously reminded everyone what to do if we were caught in the path of flying debris. The instructions were simple:

> *"WHATEVER YOU DO, DON'T RUN! PEOPLE HAVE BEEN SERIOUSLY HURT AND KILLED BECAUSE THEY RUN FROM FLYING DEBRIS AND NEVER SEE THE PIECE THAT HITS THEM FROM BEHIND. TO MAKE SURE THAT DOESN'T HAPPEN, WE MUST FACE THE EXPLOSION AND DODGE THE DEBRIS. LET'S STAY ALERT AND STAY ALIVE."*

On this particular day, in the instant I pushed the *fire* button on the blasting machine to set off one of these crater shots, I immediately knew we were in deep trouble. The marsh shot up and toward us like a fast-moving, giant wall of mud, stumps, and trees. My instant *reactive* thought was "Let's get out of here!" I was scared. I wanted to *run*; in fact, I did just that! I took off, running as fast as I could, arms and legs flailing to escape this violent explosion. About ten strides later, debris was hitting the ground around me and I realized what I was doing and how I was risking my life. In that instant, I forced myself to *stop* running and quickly turned to face the explosion and debris it hurled at me.

Clumps of mud the size of basketballs, stumps as big as chairs, and logs were raining down from the sky. For what seemed like an eternity, I scrambled around dodging the debris that otherwise could kill me. The biggest debris that fell from the sky that day was a log, about twenty-five feet long and one and a half feet in diameter. I watched it fly twenty to thirty yards over and past me.

After the terrorist attacks, I heard firemen describe what it was like running down the street, when the black cloud of debris from the World Trade Center rushed down from above and from behind them — roaring like a freight train. One described seeing big pieces of debris flying past him and I immediately thought of that day in the marsh. Fortunately, when the dust settled that day in the marsh, everyone was alive. In fact, no one had a scratch on them. We were all very shaken up and shortly thereafter, I discovered that due to miscommunication and being in a hurry to make the blast before darkness set in, we had made a major mistake. The shot was fired from one hundred feet away. Normally we fired these shots from one thousand feet away, but no one noticed in our hurried state.

My reaction to the blast is a classic example of how we *react* to Lifeblows and often take ourselves further and further from the very thing we want. Even though I had repeatedly said throughout the day, "WHATEVER YOU DO, DON'T RUN — FACE THE EXPLOSION AND DODGE THE DEBRIS —LET'S STAY ALERT AND ALIVE," my natural human reaction was to run! Even though my desire was to stay alive, my *reaction* was leading me to probable serious injury and maybe even death. My reaction was understandable; however, it was likely going to kill me. At the same instant I wanted one thing, I was generating just the opposite. Just as I had in the hospital when I wanted a close relationship with my parents, but wasn't speaking to them when they were sitting three feet away.

Something profound happened in the moments after I reacted and started running. I *noticed* my natural human reaction wasn't serving me. I noticed it could get me killed. I noticed my natural human reaction was taking me further and further from my desired outcome, so I *stopped reacting!* In the instant I turned around to face the explosion and began dodging debris, I went from *reacting* to my life challenge, to *responding* to it. I went from being out of control to in control of the outcome of staying alive. Life was no longer "happening to Bill." Bill was "happening to life."

That's the distinction between reacting and responding. When you *respond* to your Lifeblow and your life experience is based on "what I do *with* what happens to me," you are now the leader of your life. When you are happening *to* life, you are doing something *with* what has happened. In the *doing* something, you are being proactive and no longer are in the victim state. Your *response* makes you bigger than your challenge and enables you to take control of your circumstance and create happiness and fulfillment in spite of it.

The key to getting up from your personal ground zero, is NOT to *not react*. The key is to *notice* when your reaction doesn't serve you and *stop* reacting! When I realized I might kill myself, I *noticed* my reaction was keeping me from a fulfilling life. If you know what you want, you also know what you don't want. When you are in the middle of what you don't want, you have a tremendous capacity to *stop* an unhealthy reaction. However, you must be very clear about what you cherish and value and want your life and relationships to be like, as well as what you must do to create those.

The better we get at noticing when our reaction doesn't serve us, the faster we can close the gap between where we are and where we want to be. Once during a seminar, a lady asked me, "How long does it take to get it all together?" I had to smile and then suggested that she was asking the wrong person. She seemed a bit disappointed with my answer. I told her that, as far as I knew, we don't ever wake up immune to our own human reactions.

I said, "Every day I wake up, I don't welcome a flat tire. I don't plan for it, and if it happens, I'm initially upset about the inconvenience and have to do this 'responding process' all over again. Getting it all together, for me, means developing the muscle to stop harmful reactions more and more quickly."

In other words, when we are angry and upset, are we going to harmfully react for two years or two months, two weeks or two days, two hours or two minutes? Although we cannot "*not* react," we can get better and better at closing the window between when we start reacting and when we *notice* the adverse effects. The faster we *notice* our reaction taking us off track, the quicker we can *stop* the madness of thinking and acting in ways that sabotage our present moment. This is an element of time management that rarely gets attention.

Everything that ever happened in your life, happened in the *now* moment. Everything that ever happens in your life, from here on out, will happen in the *now* moment. Everything you create your life to be is done from moment to moment and each moment influences the next. This is one of the great subtleties of life. If you add enough *now* moments together, you'll be done reading this book. Tack on some more *now* moments and it will be next month. Add some more, and it will be next year. After enough *now* moments, you'll be five years older. Before you know it, you'll be so old that you forget how old you are. Don't worry, all those who know you will take great pride and find much joy in reminding you.

My point is:
Pay attention to how you're spending your now moments, and you really can't help but to notice how you are spending your life.

If you discover your reactions are costly, you can then choose to stop reacting and start responding to get more of what you want.

The next chapter gives you an opportunity to reflect on your *reaction* to the Lifeblow you identified earlier. It gives you an opportunity to acknowledge your reactions and consider how you win and how you lose when *reacting* in the ways you do. It enables you to determine if your *reactions* are costly and adversely affecting the quality of your life.

Plato said, "The beginning is the most important part of the work," and this is the beginning of the process of rising above any challenge — noticing your harmful reaction and stopping the madness of creating more reasons to be upset. **When you save *now* moments from your unhealthy and unproductive reactions, you build more productive time into your day and life.** You recapture time to create fulfillment. That's *half* the battle of "Getting Up When Life Blows You Down."

Halfway Up When Life Blows You Down

CHAPTER 3

Avoiding a Natural Disaster

"At no time in life is there a lack of opportunity to rebuild and regroup."
– Maggie Kuhn

*T*HE FLOOD EXPERIENCE I SHARED IN THE INTRODUCTION OF THIS book was my first and only experience that I would classify as a natural disaster, where Mother Nature played a role in one of my Lifeblows. Fortunately, we didn't have any belongings worth a lot of money, so we didn't lose what we would have lost if we had had the same experience later in life. Yet there was still a sense of loss associated with our flooded apartment. Our books were ruined and final exams were a few weeks away. Our furniture and belongings were destroyed. We temporarily lost our home, property, comfort, and peace of mind. Fortunately, we didn't lose our four-legged best friends.

Whenever I hear about natural disasters in the news, I think back to 1983 when I was flooded out of that little apartment in New Orleans and the victim of a natural disaster. Regardless of whether a natural disaster is a hurricane, landslide, earthquake, forest fire, volcano, tornado, blizzard, or flood, most of the stories we hear include reports about people who have lost something. If people don't lose their life, they lose their property, jobs, productive time, health, money, homes, family members, friends, and part of themselves — their hopes, dreams, and positive outlook. They lose their experience of peace, happiness, and fulfillment. They lose their sense of security.

Not long ago, I realized that with my natural human reaction to Lifeblows, I've lost all the things that people lose in natural disasters.

I've lost property when I've gotten mad and thrown something and broken it. I've lost my health when I've let life happen to me to the degree I experience an enormous amount of stress from being out of control. I've lost money when I've gotten upset with a person and reacted in a way they use as a reason to not do business. I once lost a relationship when I fired someone in the heat of the moment and later regretted it. When I was in the hospital, I lost relationships with my mom and dad and some friends. Not because they died, but because my reaction to my Lifeblow gave me a *right* to give them the silent treatment and our connection died. I lost productive time. I lost a big part of myself while beating myself up, criticizing my actions, calling myself stupid, and lowering my self-esteem. With my negative thoughts about myself and my situation — I lost peace of mind, fulfillment, joy, happiness, and hope that tomorrow could be better. **Everything that can be lost in a natural disaster from Mother Nature can be lost in a natural human reaction!**

Not only did my Lifeblow of being robbed and shot teach me that, so did my Lifeblow of going through a divorce several years ago. Consider my reactions leading up to that outcome. While I was still married and working on improving my relationship with my wife, on occasion I would come home from work and my wife and I would have a disagreement about something. An example would be my getting home later than I had expected and told her before leaving that morning. When such things happened, she'd get upset and frustrated, particularly when plans we'd made were ruined. When she expressed her upset, I would take her comments as criticism, never considering that her upset might be due to her worrying if I was okay. My five hundred words per minute of reactive thinking included:

> *"This is baloney. I couldn't do a thing about being late. I've just worked a fifteen-hour day and coming home should be a nice experience — not one that's less friendly than work. I don't need this. I shouldn't have to put up with it. Since when am I the only one who messes up and 'mis-plans' sometimes?"* and on and on . . .

The reactive feelings these thoughts generated were *anger and frustration*, and my reactive action (reaction) was to *storm off to our second bedroom, close the door, and play possum.* I wanted to avoid the conflict.

By the way, I remember being so *right* about my reaction. As you might expect, this behavior didn't solve a thing. It only created more anger, frustration, and resentment. Our issues of conflict grew bigger and bigger, eventually getting to the point where more arguing became eminent. Whenever it happened, I'd always wind up behind that closed door, stewing about my predicament. Over time, this routine repeated itself more frequently. Communication shut down and, likewise, the less I talked, the more I built a wall between us. We were coexisting under one roof. Living together, but alone. I made her the culprit for all the problems we were having. I made her the cause of all our unhappiness. I made her wrong and myself *right* about the condition of our marriage.

This went on for months. The stress mounted. My blood pressure soared. I remember going to work and my friends, who knew we were having trouble, would ask me how my marriage was doing. My answer was always the same, "It's horrible," and I would go on to complain about how miserable I was, hoping and wishing that it would somehow get better. I was living at the lowest form of human existence, waiting for someone else to do something to make a positive difference in my life. Talk about clueless. I was complaining about my awful marriage, yet I was the stubborn, uncommunicative husband contributing daily and greatly to its demise.

The outcome was inevitable. We got divorced. I lost my marriage. I lost my home. I lost my confidence. I lost my peace of mind. I lost my health. I lost a friend. Although my ex-wife and I are good friends today, my point here is that I subconsciously reacted the same way I did after being shot and after the explosion. In the case of my marriage, however, I never stopped my reaction to open up a new possibility for the relationship. My natural reaction created a natural disaster. I lost the same things I could have lost in a flood, hurricane, or mudslide. Once we acknowledge the cost of our natural human reactions, we can take steps to prevent our natural reactions from becoming natural disasters.

Ensuring that our natural reactions to Lifeblows never create or become natural disasters — means noticing *how* and *when* our reactions don't serve us. The only difference in losing a loved one in a hurricane and losing a loved one when we react to conflict and say hurtful words is that we have a choice about the latter. There are too many people moving on to try to meet the right person, instead of becoming the right person with a new set of choices. We may not be able to stop a hurricane, but we can certainly stop ourselves from blowing up and creating stormy relationships that eventually *blow* our marriage away.

The exercise that follows will invite you to take a very close look at yourself and help you identify your *reactions* to your Lifeblow, as well as the *outcomes* and *consequences* of those reactions. You may find the process fun, difficult, threatening, uncomfortable, enlightening, confronting, challenging, wonderful, or tedious. One thing is for sure: At the end of the process, you will be ready to continue with the remainder of the book, trash it, or set it aside for another day. Acknowledging negativity and its consequences is something many people don't want to do, much less begin to work on. Thomas Edison said, "Opportunity is missed by most people because it's dressed in overalls and looks like work." This applies to your opportunity to experience fulfillment after any Lifeblow. It'll take some work.

Rising above challenges, demands that this work be part of the process. Just remember that the only purpose of this exercise is to ultimately help you create a much more fulfilling life than your reactions to your Lifeblow are allowing at this time.

1. NOTICING YOUR REACTION TO YOUR LIFEBLOW

Stopping unhealthy reactions begins with noticing how you talk to yourself after your Lifeblow. As you become aware of your thoughts, notice some of the reactive signs in your language. When we react, we often use a lot of "all-ness" words, absolute phrases such as all, none, never, always, and forever. My reaction included, "*All* my effort has been wasted. I'll *never* feel safe again. I'll *always* wonder about people. *No one* can be trusted.

In addition, our reactive thoughts also include "must" words, such as should, shouldn't, should have, could have, mustn't, must, and have to. "I *shouldn't* have been at the ATM so early. I *could have* waited to get money. I *have to* get revenge for what the robber did to me."

Once your reactive thoughts are identified, notice how *right* and justified you are and how you feel when you say these things to yourself.

a. The following are general reactive thoughts that follow Lifeblows. Do you recognize any of these thoughts?

- What's the world coming to?
- I don't deserve this.
- I can't believe this is happening.
- I'm sick of getting the short end of the stick.
- I always seem to get picked.
- Why me?
- Things never go right.
- Why am I always the one?
- I can't trust anyone.
- It's always something.
- Things never work out.
- This makes me so mad!
- Just my luck.
- I'm such an idiot. Will I ever learn?
- I'll never be safe again.
- I never get a break.
- This whole thing is so depressing.
- Nothing ever seems to go right for me.
- When it rains, it pours.
- Poor me.
- Life's not fair.
- I didn't ask for this.
- What will everyone think of me?
- All my effort has been wasted.
- My life is screwed up forever.
- I'll never recover.
- No one will want me.
- This is impossible.
- If I had only known.

b. Think carefully about what it's like for you in the midst or aftermath of your Lifeblow. How would you rate yourself on a scale of one (very little) to five (most intense), in defining the strength of what you are experiencing.

- Anger
- Frustration
- Being Afraid
- Helplessness
- Hopelessness
- Feeling Abused
- Hatefulness
- Betrayal
- Being Destroyed
- Shock
- Being Cheated
- Feeling Stupid
- Disappointment
- Feeling Sorry for self
- Discouragement
- Resentment
- Distrust
- Being Violated
- Hurt
- Depression

c. Become aware of how your thoughts and feelings cause you to react. Based on what you identified in "b," how would you complete the following sentence? (Apply this sentence to everything you are experiencing and identified above.)

Because I feel _____, I therefore find myself

_____

_____

(behavior and actions)

The following questions are here for you to further become aware of your automatic reaction to your Lifeblow, where those reactions leave you, and how they impact the quality of your life. As you answer, allow your feelings to rise up.

1. With regard to my feelings, am I entitled to feel this way?
2. What activities am I planning in order to deal with this situation?
3. What activities am I engaged in to resolve this issue?
4. How am I spending my time while dealing with my challenge?
5. When do I think about my Lifeblow?
6. With whom and how do I talk about this issue? How does that affect my relationship with people?
7. Where do I think about and work on this issue?
8. If my Lifeblow never happened, how would I be spending my time?
9. Can I "un-do" the Lifeblow that happened?
10. When I am finished doing what I do or have planned to do, where will I be?
11. How long will this process take?
12. Are my actions, or planned actions, hurting anyone?
13. Are my actions, or planned actions, inadvertently hurting anyone?
14. Who are my actions hurting?
15. How do I feel about hurting other people?
16. Am I out for revenge?
17. Is the revenge I seek, consistent with my faith?
18. Is the revenge I seek, consistent with my values?
19. Are my actions or planned actions legal?
20. If not, what are the consequences? Am I ready to face them?
21. Is my family ready to face them?
22. Will I be changing the fact that "What's done is done"?
23. Am I building relationships?
24. Am I tearing relationships down?
25. Am I making friends?
26. Am I losing friends?

27. Am I adversely affecting my business, job, or career?
28. Am I sabotaging anything I value? If so, what?
29. Am I adversely affecting my dreams?
30. Am I adversely affecting my family?
31. Am I adversely affecting my financial situation?
32. Am I adversely affecting my health and well-being?
33. If I keep my actions up, will my Lifeblow go away?
34. Do my attitude and actions improve the quality of my life and relationships?
35. Am I being controlled by my Lifeblow? Is life "happening to me"?
36. Do I like to be controlled?
37. Does my experience "make me" mad, resentful, frustrated, upset, disappointed, and discouraged?
38. Do I enjoy being forced to feel a certain way and behave in a certain manner?

2. IDENTIFY THE CONSEQUENCES OF YOUR REACTION

After becoming aware of my reactions to being shot at the ATM, I realized the consequences of my reactions — listed below. On one hand, with my reaction to being shot — I won in certain ways. I gained something. On the other hand, I also lost in certain ways. I paid a price for my reaction.

Now it is your turn to continue the process of creating fulfillment in spite of your Lifeblow. Consider the two lists that follow. The first list is of how you benefit (what you get/gain) from your reactions. The second is of how you pay a price (what you lose) because of your reactions. Also, think about other ways you win/lose that aren't listed.

How I Win	How I Lose
__ I get to "be right" about my thoughts, feelings, and actions	__ I waste precious time
	__ I waste energy and feel drained
__ I get to complain	__ I am not as productive as I could be
__ I get to be defensive	
__ I get to feel powerful when I'm defensive	__ I do nothing/very little constructive
__ I get to throw a pity party!	__ I contribute little worthwhile to people
__ I get to plan revenge	
__ I get sympathy from people	__ I help no one
__ I get to even the score	__ My dream dies
__ I get to blame others	__ Personal and business relationships suffer
__ I get to make excuses	
__ I get to feel justified about my anger and upset	__ I don't keep or make friends
	__ My health and well being suffer
__ Others	__ I don't experience love, happiness, peace, joy, fulfillment, vitality, or intimacy
	__ People don't want to be around me
	__ My finances suffer
	__ I live in the past instead of the present
	__ I'm being controlled and am out of control
	__ I miss opportunities
	__ I don't grow as a person
	__ I don't laugh much
	__ I feel dead inside
	__ I lose self esteem
	__ I compromise my values
	__ I'm a victim of my circumstance
	__ Others

3. Determine if My Reaction Costs Me More Than It's Worth

After I took an inventory of my *reactions* and realized how they were costing me things such as fulfillment, happiness, and close relationships with family and friends, I immediately knew that I could do one of two things. I could continue *reacting* in the same way and continue creating more misery for myself *or stop reacting* and start looking for ways to *respond* to my challenge and recapture the things I had lost by reacting. It became clear that the quality of my life was at stake with my decision.

Consider the consequences of your reaction to your Lifeblow and ask yourself the following questions:

1. Am I paying a serious price for my reaction?
2. Is my reaction costing me more than it's worth?
3. Do my reactions prevent me from experiencing and creating the life that I desire?

If your answers to the above questions are NO, your *reaction* to your challenge is not adversely affecting the quality of your life, at least not enough to make any changes. If your answers to the above questions are YES, you have determined that your *reaction* to your Lifeblow is negatively impacting the quality of your life, and you will want to continue by answering the following question:

"DO I WANT TO STOP LIVING LIKE THIS?"

I was once asked the following question after a speech:

"When does a Lifeblow go from being an experience that generates a natural human negative reaction, to an excuse for not living life fully?"

At the time, I didn't really have an answer to that question. I thought it was a great question, but who am I to be the judge for how long anyone, including myself, should react to a Lifeblow? Newspaper headlines on September 24, 2001, said, "<u>Official Mourning</u>

Period Ends." We all know that mourning the outcome of the terrorist attacks didn't end for most people on that day. It would be completely unrealistic for someone else to dictate the length of such a process. In other words, it would be absurd for me to say something like, "Well, if you get robbed and shot at an ATM, you should be over it in two months, thirteen days, four hours, and eighteen minutes." That's ridiculous. We'll never get over some Lifeblows, only past them with a fulfilling or unfulfilling life. In light of all that, however, there's still the very good question, *"When does a Lifeblow go from being an experience that generates a natural human negative reaction, to an excuse for not living life fully?"*

Those headlines on September 24, 2001, "Official Mourning Period Ends," announced that as a nation, we were now going to move forward and RESPOND to create a brighter future in spite of the terrorist attacks. In creating that day, our leadership was reminding us of Mark Twain's quote that "Life goes on," and as a nation, we will do just that. As it turns out, it was a very good idea that got a lot of support, and ultimately helped all of us.

When interviewed about his thoughts playing against the Atlanta Braves in the first regular season game in New York since the attacks, New York Mets Manager Bobby Valentine said, "I feel without a doubt that it's good for the healing process. We'll show our city that we're trying to win a battle against fear, and that's what we can do." That spirit was echoed by baseball fans in New York, one saying, "I'm ready for some baseball. We've got to show we are going to move forward and this is the national pastime."

International Olympic Committee President Jacques Rogge, who had unilateral power to cancel the Olympic Games in Salt Lake City, said, "The Olympic Games will go on. They are an answer to the current violence and should not be a victim of that." Allen Steinfeld, race director for the 26th running of the NYC Marathon on November 4, 2001, told a reporter, "The race will go on. This year's race will be a validation of our spirit beyond words. The race has always been about highlighting diversity and energy. This year another word gets added, "resilience" — of New York City and New Yorkers."

When players on the New York Giants visited rescue workers at Ground Zero, they received a loud and clear message from those heroes, "Play on!"

After thinking about that initial question: *"When does a Lifeblow go from being an experience that generates a natural human negative reaction, to an excuse for not living life fully?"* I came up with an answer that is in line with what rescue workers expressed. It doesn't speak to the grieving and healing process, but rather to the progress we make <u>while</u> grieving and healing. My answer to the above question is, *"As soon as we are willing/able to see it that way."* If you have gone through the process in this chapter and determined that your reaction costs you dearly, then perhaps now you can view your Lifeblow as an excuse you may have used for not living life fully — and decide to play on.

A few years ago I attended a seminar conducted by motivational speaker, Zig Ziglar, and as an audience member was asked four questions that I invite you to answer here for yourself.

---

1. *Is there something I can do in the next twenty-four hours that will make my life worse?*

2. *Is there something I can do in the next twenty-four hours that will make my life better?*

3. *Do I have a choice in the matter of my life?*

4. *Does every choice I make have an end result?*

After asking these questions, Ziglar then said, "If you answered YES to this series of questions, whether or not you realize it, here's what you just said:

"No matter how good or bad my past is, no matter how good or bad my present situation is, there is something I can do in the next twenty-four hours that will make my future, either better or worse, and the choice is mine.'"

I'll add that *now* is the time to exercise your choice to improve your life. Seneca said, "One should count each day a separate life." There is immense wisdom in that. I learned from being shot, and we all learned from the terrorist attacks, that we are living moment to moment to moment to moment, and have no idea what is going to happen in the next one. I turned around to say good morning and was in the middle of a robbery. All of us woke up after the terrorists struck and quickly found ourselves in the middle of America under attack, not knowing where the next plane would hit or who we might know at the place when it did. We truly don't know what the "tomorrow morning of our life" might bring.

Given that, I believe it's important to ask questions like, "If life as I know it, ended tomorrow — how am I living my life today? How happy am I? How fulfilled am I? What have I accomplished? Am I accomplishing everything I'd like in the important areas of career, finances, relationships, and health? Am I making progress in the areas of my life that I value and cherish and matter the most?" These are important questions to consider. **There is no conference table in any town, city, county, state, or country on the planet, where there is a group of people sitting around right now trying to figure out how to make *your life* better.**

If you don't direct the spotlight of awareness inward, nobody else will. If you don't become aware of your reaction to your challenges, and look closely at how they impact the quality of your life, nobody else will. If you don't *stop* reactions that are detrimental to having the life you want, nobody else will. It's up to you to take responsibility for how you have/are contributing to the life you've created.

Fulfillment in life begins in the instant you do more than you have to and understand why you are doing it. Operating in your reactive mode will give you everything you *need* to survive in life. By the way, a homeless man will also get everything he needs to survive — he'll get food, he'll get water, and he'll get shelter if he needs them badly enough. On the other hand, it's the things in life you *want* that require discipline to do the "extra" things. Ordinary people react and get what they *need*. Extraordinary people respond and get what they *want* because they *notice* and *stop* harmful reactions that take them off track.

I have a friend who had a major disagreement with his father. My friend was angry and hurt, and decided his father owed him an apology. After any disagreement, my friend was always the one to say, "I'm sorry," but now he wasn't going to give in to his father so easily. He was sick of his dad not ever admitting any wrongdoing, and he was going to call him to say that if they were going to have a relationship, it would be up to his dad to make an apology. My friend was "being *right*" about his opinion and "making his dad wrong." After discussing this situation with my friend, he saw how a verbal attack on his father was going to drive a bigger wedge in their relationship. Reminding his dad that he was a jerk held little possibility for making amends and creating the close relationship they both silently longed for.

Long story short, my friend decided to take the higher road by *not* calling his father to give him a piece of his mind. He saw how much more damaging that would be to their relationship. In effect, he *stopped* his reaction *toward* his father. He was still being *right* about his opinion of what happened, but not further damaging the relationship and broadening the chasm. He wanted to collect himself and make sure he didn't make things worse. My friend was preventing a natural disaster with his dad by taking time out to accept responsibility and give some thought to what he wanted to create their relationship to be. It would be <u>very</u> important that my friend not let this non-communication routine go on for too long. He might take himself out of his relationship with his dad long enough to create distance, discomfort, and resentment, perfect ingredients to create a natural disaster.

Going back to the question, relative to your harmful reactions that cost you more than you'd like, "DO I WANT TO STOP LIVING LIKE THIS?"

If your answer is NO, suffering is an option. There is nothing wrong with your choice. After all, it's your freedom and your life. The only other thing I would suggest is to notice your most common complaints about your life. Then look to see if your complaint is fueled in some way by what you create with your reaction to your Lifeblow. If you have a complaint and the complaint persists, there is a reason. Your complaint means that it is important to you that something changes. You care too much about what you are complaining about. Indifference doesn't complain. You wouldn't complain if you didn't care. You wouldn't complain if the source of your complaint didn't matter to you.

Karen Lamb said, "A year from now, you may wish you had started today."

If your Lifeblow reaction is part of the source of your complaint, the most available source of change is your choice to *stop* your reaction today and shut down the source of your discontent. You can choose to react and you can choose to stop reacting; therefore it is absurd to complain about the choices you make.

If you don't choose to stop reacting, at least stop complaining.

If your answer is YES to the question, "Do I want to stop living like this?" — Dr. Seuss would be applauding. He said, "You have brains in your head and feet in your shoes. You can steer yourself any direction you choose." You've acknowledged that status quo is no longer acceptable, and that you are ready to do what it takes to start creating the fulfilling life you want. With the choice to *stop* your reaction to your challenge, you've hunkered down and are starting to regroup. You have positioned yourself to redirect your harmful reactive energy in a way that lifts you up and enables you to soar toward a more fulfilling life. You are avoiding a natural disaster.

Abe Lincoln said, "Most people are about as happy as they make up their minds to be." Congratulations for making up your mind to *stop* your harmful reactive humanness and making up your mind to be happy! You are winning the first *half* of the battle of "Getting Up When Life Blows You Down."

CHAPTER 4

Committing to the Rest of Your Journey Up

"Commitment is the first step, and all else lines up"
– Sir Edmund Hillary, Mountain Climber

R ISING ABOVE ANY LIFEBLOW BEGINS WITH A COMMITMENT TO engage in a process. The word commitment can be bothersome when associated with personal change. Committing to something often sounds like a threat to freedom, happiness and the ability to enjoy life. Granted, sometimes that is true, but it all depends on who or what you are committing to and why. On the journey of "creating fulfillment after your challenge," the key is committing to the process presented in this book. Being committed, or not, will have a great deal to do with what you get out of this book, so let's take a look at how making a commitment can help when you set out to "Get Up When Life Blows You Down."

Imagine that you and I take a walk every morning, part of which includes strolling along the banks of a river. This portion of the walk is our favorite. Along the way, we take in the sounds of rushing water and singing birds. We crunch through the yellow, red and orange leaves that have fallen the season before. For some reason, the air smells better here. It seems to be forever moving, carrying with it the fragrance of various plants and flowers. The breeze is cool and always accompanied by the sound of rustling leaves on streamside trees that turn the ground into a myriad of moving shadows.

Weeks pass and on one particular day, you and I make a commitment to one another to cross the river. We walk along the same path we have been taking for months, retracing our footsteps from weeks past, until we find ourselves beside the river. As we walk along, the beauty and serenity are all present, but for some reason, we aren't noticing *that* aspect of our walk today. The walk along the river is very different today. Our conversation and experience during our walk is unlike any we have ever had before.

You point out a rock in the river and say, "Bill, maybe we can wade out to that rock and then climb up and jump over to that fallen tree."

Then I say, "Yes, and it looks like we can walk across the fallen tree and get over to where that flat rock is. From there, maybe we can swim to that overhanging branch and use it to pull ourselves toward that other group of rocks. . . ."

You nod your head and all of the sudden say, "But wait. Look down there. Does it look to you that maybe the river narrows downstream at the bend in the river? Maybe we should walk down there and see if there may be an easier way. . . ."

We are noticing aspects of the river that we never noticed before. For months, we didn't care how close any rock might be to a fallen tree, but today that information means everything. The fallen trees and rocks are much more than fallen trees and rocks; they are stepping stones for crossing the river. Isn't this interesting? The river hasn't changed one iota. You and I haven't changed either. The trees and rocks are the same, but our entire experience of walking along the river has been transformed.

The only difference between our walk today and our previous walks is that we decided we wanted to end up in a different place on this day and then made a <u>commitment</u> to get there. Our goal and our commitment to cross the river has not only transformed our experience, it's also created a new possibility for our life. Our goal and commitment give us a sense of direction, as well as the ability to notice and act on pertinent information for accomplishing our objective.

Just as your relationship with a river is transformed when you decide what you want and commit to getting there, your relationship with your Lifeblow can be transformed when you do the same thing. Your commitment to the process in this book will enable you to notice things as you read that you would not otherwise notice. They will be stepping-stones for you and will help you along your journey of "Getting Up When Life Blows You Down."

In making this kind of commitment, you are committing yourself to a worthwhile effort. Being committed to something or simply being involved in it are two very different ways to bring yourself to the life you lead. My experience shows that the outcomes are also significantly different. If you consider how different a relationship will turn out, depending on whether you are involved with someone or committed to them, you begin to understand the significant advantage a commitment gives you. It's like a glue that creates an important mindset of stick-to-it-ness, which has much to do with the success of your endeavor.

Our commitment is not unlike the commitment a firefighter makes when he or she takes the oath to save lives. Their commitment is what enables them to risk their lives to save others. Their commitment to humanity was what had them running up the stairs while encouraging and helping everyone else to evacuate the World Trade Center. Their commitment is what kept them engaged in the task at hand, instead of escaping, as many people did who had not made the same commitment. Their commitment is what enabled them to work around the clock for days in the rescue effort after the collapse of the World Trade Center.

When one of the firemen, who was trapped in the collapse of the towers, was found and recovered, his commitment shone through when he refused to go to the hospital. He wanted to stay and search for others like him, saying, "We will keep going and not dishonor the people who may be still alive or who have lost their lives." Being committed, really committed, to something important to you, gives you the same kind of drive and resiliency demonstrated by that fireman. Just as a fireman's commitment brings forth extraordinary results, your commitment to the process in this book will help you to do the same, in the aftermath of your Lifeblow.

Now that you've identified your Lifeblow and really become "present" to what took place, how you feel, and how you are spending your time, consider the following passage. If "Commitment" was a person who could talk — here's what it would say and ask about your time together:

The Invitation

It doesn't interest me what you do for a living. I want to know what you ache for and if you dare to dream of meeting your heart's longing.

It doesn't interest me how old you are. I want to know if you will risk looking like a fool for love, for your dream, for the adventure of being alive.

It doesn't interest me what planets are squaring your moon. I want to know if you have touched the center of your own sorrow, if you have been opened by life's betrayals, or have shriveled and closed from fear of further pain. I want to know if you can sit with pain, mine or your own, without moving to hide it or fake it or fix it. I want to know if you can be with joy, mine or your own; if you can dance with wildness and let the ecstasy fill you to the tips of your fingers and toes without cautioning us to be careful, realistic, or to remember the limitations of being human.

It doesn't interest me if the story you're telling is true. I want to know if you can disappoint another to be true to yourself; if you can bear the accusation of betrayal and not betray your own soul. I want to know if you can be faithful and therefore be trustworthy. I want to know if you can see beauty everyday, even when it is not pretty, and if you can source your life on the edge of the lake and shout to the silver of the full moon, "YES!"

It doesn't interest me to know where you live or how much money you have. I want to know if you can get up after a night of grief and despair, wary and bruised to the bone, and do what needs to be done.

It doesn't interest me to know who you know or how you came to be here. I want to know if you will stand in the center of the fire with me and not shrink back.

It doesn't interest me where or what or with whom you have studied. I want to know what sustains you from the inside when all else falls away. I want to know if you can be alone with yourself and if you truly like the company you keep in the empty moments.

– Oriah Mountain Dreamer, 1999

The above passage contains many descriptors of what our lives can be like after a Lifeblow hits. I guarantee that committing to the process of this book, by internalizing and acting on what you read here, will enable you to answer YES to everything "Commitment" wants to know in The Invitation. That's my promise to you.

Are you willing to commit to the journey ahead? Are you ready to make a commitment to be fulfilled, no matter what, in the aftermath of your Lifeblows — including the one you are dealing with now? If so, give your word to yourself that you will do whatever it is you have to do, in the context of your daily life, to "Get Up When Life Blows You Down" and reach your new plateau in life.

My favorite definition of commitment is, "Doing what you said you would do, long after the moment in which you said it, has passed." The next step is to sign your name to the agreement you are making with yourself. "Signing off" on what you say you'll do, gives you an advantage to follow through, l–o–n–g after this very moment. Any casually set goal is easily abandoned at the first sign of an obstacle. Since signing a marriage certificate, business contract, school registration papers, or an employment agreement, improves the chances for "doing what we said we'd do, long after the moment in which we said it, has passed" — we can make that "glue" work here too.

Take out a piece of paper, write down your commitment to "Get Up When Life Blows You Down," and sign your name and the date.

School never taught us of the importance or power of making agreements with ourselves to stand for things that produce extraordinary results in life. Life would be a lot different if the only things in the middle of the road were a yellow line and a dead possum. Magic happens when you stand for something. For whatever it's worth, producing an extraordinary result in spite of your Lifeblow starts right here, in your stand for the good life.

On a separate piece of paper, write the following, fill in the blanks, sign, and post it where you will see it everyday — refrigerator, bathroom mirror:

I _____(your name)_____ fully commit to do whatever I have to do, in order to experience happiness and fulfillment in the aftermath of my Lifeblow.

_____(signature)_____   ____(date)____

In the words of Abraham Lincoln: "Always bear in mind that your own resolution to succeed is more important than any other one thing." You've just made such a resolution with yourself.

If you initially read the subtitle of this book and wondered why it is called *11 ½ Ways to Get Up and Thrive When the Winds of Change Howl*, the mystery is over. I used a play on words, or numbers, to make a very important point. The "1/2 Ways" actually represents "Being Halfway" along your journey to fulfillment. When you notice your costly reactions and *stop* them because of the toll they take on the quality of your life, and then secure yourself in your progress up by making a commitment to go the rest of the way, you've won half the battle for a more fulfilling life. You are HALF-WAY UP WHEN LIFE BLOWS YOU DOWN.

What's left are the 11 ways to go the rest of the way — 11 Ways to get all the way up — to stand tall with a smile on your face, regardless of your tough circumstances. Before I get into the specific 11 Ways, it's helpful to have some understanding for how we operate as human beings. After covering that in the following segment, Part 4 will cover the 11 Ways I "Got Up and Thrived" after the shooting. Part 4 will cover how I slowly but surely created "Being robbed and shot," into "THE BEST THING THAT EVER HAPPENED TO ME."

If, after waking up after my first surgery, you had told me, "Bill, being shot is going to be a great experience for you!" I probably would have tried to wrap my hands around your neck so I could start squeezing. Obviously at that time, getting robbed and shot was, without a doubt, the worst thing I could have ever imagined. Although my ATM experience is *still* the worst experience I've had to date, today it also represents a great gift that has significantly added to my life. The reason for that is because it initiated *a process*, which has led me to where I am today — more happy and fulfilled than I've ever been at any other time in my life. I don't want to get shot again so that I repeat the process and learn more life-lessons, but I wouldn't trade the experience for anything for how it has positively contributed to my life.

Your challenge holds that possibility. I'm not suggesting that one day you will see your Lifeblow as "the best thing that ever happened." That might not be remotely possible for many reasons.

What is possible, however, is that your experience also initiates a process that ultimately adds a lot of value and fulfillment to your life, in the aftermath of your Lifeblow.

From here on out, take the appropriate time to become absorbed in the information that follows. Constantly bring yourself to the message on each page, searching for ways to apply it to your life. If you do that, fulfillment will be your reward. Engage in this process for yourself, no one else. Honor your word. Honor the commitment you have made to go the rest of the way. Here we go!

PART THREE

Ready to Stand Tall after Your Lifeblow

CHAPTER 5

When the Truth Won't Set You Free

"I'm not so sure about what I've been so sure about."

WELCOME TO THE SECOND HALF OF YOUR JOURNEY OF "GETTING Up When Life Blows You Down"! Before Mother Theresa died, she visited San Quentin Prison. While addressing the prisoners, she drew a circle, like the one below, on a board.

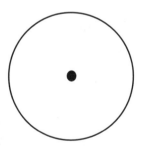

Pointing to the dot in the middle of the circle, Mother Theresa addressed the prisoners and said, "This dot represents your 'smirchment' against society." Then she gestured to the space outside the dot and said, "And this space represents the infinite potential on the canvas called your life."

Mother Theresa was talking about "becoming more" as a human being. Although the context is different, her diagram and message are one to take to heart and apply if we are going to rise above setbacks. Our *reactive* ways represent the dot in Mother Theresa's circle. The dot represents who you have become, with your natural human reaction, as a result of your Lifeblow. George Eliot said, "It's never too late to be who you might have been." Progress outward from the dot and into the space in the circle representing "your infinite potential," is a journey. It's a journey of *growth*. It's a journey of *change*. It's a journey that asks you to "*become* more today than you were yesterday." It's a journey of a leader, a leader of one's life and in one's life to create a brighter tomorrow. Leaders don't wake up after a Lifeblow, and look outside and groan, "How in the world am I going to make it through this day?" Leaders of their life, wake up and look out at the same day, and then lift their head and square their shoulders, and ask, "Who am I going to *become* today?"

Becoming more as a human being, can involve many things. For me, it means having an objective that you are growing toward. In this case, that objective is being fulfilled and creating desired outcomes when you have a Lifeblow.

Reaching that objective means making new choices about how we think and behave — purposeful choices that are designed to take us to a new and meaningful plateau. Becoming more means living life outside of your comfort zone; in other words, thinking and doing things that are new and that you weren't thinking or doing yesterday, last week, or last month. Miguel De Cervantes said, "Get the better of yourself — this is the best kind of victory." With your choice to stop your Lifeblow reaction, you have already become more as a person. By committing to the rest of the process, you've gotten the better of yourself.

The message in this book is one of becoming even more now. Its focus is on changing your life by exploring your belief system, noting the kind of life experience your beliefs bring you, and intentionally making shifts in those perspectives about your Lifeblow, that do nothing but keep you down and upset.

All of us have a belief system, made up of what we think are truths about ourselves, other people, the world, and our circumstances. Since all of our reactions are driven by that belief system, "Getting Up When Life Blows You Down" requires challenging your belief system and changing it, where necessary, to transform your life.

Before we continue, let's take a minute to better understand how we develop our belief system, or what I also call THE TRUTH we hold about ourselves, other people, and the world. A few years ago I remember standing in front of a big window, looking into the nursery at a hospital where friends of mine had just had their first baby. As I looked into that room at my friends' newborn son, along with another dozen or so babies, the thought that occurred to me was, "At this very moment, all of these babies have the same chance to fulfill their God-given potential."

In his book *The Self-Talk Solution*, Shad Helmstetter draws a wonderful analogy between our mind and a record. He says, "We are all born with a nice, clean, shiny record, on which nothing has ever been recorded. As soon as we're born, the needle comes down on our record and starts cutting grooves in the record. With each passing day, every word we hear and every thought we think, about every experience we have, cuts a groove in the record. The words and thoughts that are repeated over and over again, cut grooves that become deeper and more permanent. The deeper, more permanent grooves represent our conditioned-in beliefs and attitudes, or *truth* about ourselves, other people, and the world."

All of us have *truths* about everything and everybody. When older adults think of teenagers, there are many automatic *truths* that automatically arise in their thinking. They have a "teenage *truth*" — "They are loud, unruly, rebellious, clueless, listen to stupid music, and drive fast." When teenagers think of older adults, the same thing happens. Teenagers have automatic "old folk *truths*" such as, "They are boring, demanding, listen to stupid music, and drive way to slow."

Our *truths* dictate how we feel and act, and our actions dictate our life results — good or bad, positive or negative, constructive or destructive, and encouraging or discouraging, leaving us happy or unhappy and fulfilled or unfulfilled. Simply said, everything we create is a result of what we hold as our *truth*. If we create a disaster after a Lifeblow, it's because we have a *truth* that automatically leads to a specific set of actions that cause disaster. If our *truth* were different, our actions would be different, and so would our outcome.

Let's go back to my experience of looking into the nursery at the group of newborn babies. In the moment I was observing them, none of those miracles of God had any *truths*. They had no biases, beliefs, or prejudices. In the words of Shad Helmstetter, "They had no cluttered notions in their mind about what is right or what is wrong and what works or doesn't work. They had no likes or dislikes, no political points of view, no conditioning whatsoever." They had their lives in front of them, taking no attitudes or beliefs into their future. They were peaceful, trusting, joyful, unconditionally loving, and full of acceptance for all human beings. In a few days, upon leaving the hospital, they would willingly go home with *anyone* who would take them. However, the babies aren't taken home by just anyone. My friends took their son home and the other babies presumably went home with their parents, natural or otherwise. It was from their "home" that all these babies would begin to experience life and begin to develop their *truths* about themselves, other people, and the world.

Said another way, they would begin to be conditioned. With each passing day, as they grew older, they would begin learning from their environment, experiences, and the people in their world. When a baby is taken home, they experience how people talk to and treat one another. They experience how people talk to and treat them. They begin learning about the world and the people in it, from their environment and observations. The world is their teacher. A young child learns to hate the exact same way he or she learns that $1 + 1 = 2$. In either case, a thought gets planted and the child repeats it over and over until it becomes that child's *truth*.

Young children are like sponges, absorbing all they can from any source. They are full of questions. Sometimes they ask them and sometimes they don't, but they always have them, and they always find answers for themselves. Have you ever noticed how many questions, kids ask? They learn each and every time they receive answers to their questions. They get answers to their questions: *what, when, where, why, how,* and *who,* and start developing a belief system. They learn from and are taught by their parents, siblings, neighbors, and conversations they overhear the ice cream truck driver having on his cell phone while giving them their change.

When they get to school age, they learn from teachers, classmates, and experiences they have on the playground. When they are five, they learn from the thirteen-year-old down the street. They learn from coaches, ministers, rabbis, mentors, and messages picked up from television, radio, video games, magazines, and newspapers. Helmstetter went on to say, "Collectively, every word they hear and every thought they think, about every experience they have, will lead to their *truth* about themselves, the world, and everyone in it."

One of my favorite little stories that shows how we are conditioned, is the one about the little girl who used to ride to school with her dad every morning. This went on for weeks, until one day her father was out of town on business and her mom took her to school. On the way, after about fifteen minutes of driving, the little girl asked her mom, "Where are all the bastards today?"

Surprised at her daughter's language and question, Mom asked, "What do you mean? Where did you hear that word?"

It all made sense when her daughter said, "Well, I'm just wondering where they all are. When I ride to school with Daddy, we've seen at least five or six of them by now."

I saw a great example of our human conditioning while watching a special on TV with Peter Jennings. The program was aired to answer the questions children had about the terrorist attacks. There was a room full of children, ages five to fifteen, along with a few adults who would help answer questions and support the conversation as needed. During the program, one five-year-old little girl asked, "Why did it happen? I just don't understand? Why would someone do this? How can people hate people they don't know?"

Following her questions, Peter Jennings asked the other children, "Does anyone know why someone would do this?" A few hands were raised, and Jennings called on a boy who was about fourteen.

The boy proceeded to answer by saying, "Muslims worship a different God than us, and the Muslim Bible teaches that if you kill someone, you will go to heaven."

After allowing a few more kids a chance to express their thoughts, Jennings directed his attention to a Muslim religious man, who was part of the audience, and asked him to comment. This man began sharing Muslim beliefs with the children, including the fact that Muslims worship the same God who is worshiped in the Christian and Jewish faiths. He helped the kids understand that Christians in the Middle East refer to God as Allah, NOT because the God is different. The name they give God is different because the language and culture are different. He informed these very impressionable minds that the Muslim religion and Koran (the Muslim "Bible") promotes peace among fellow human beings and that nowhere, does it encourage killing or suggest that people can kill other people and go to heaven.

In that very brief exchange, we saw a great example of how we are all conditioned differently. The teenager, who thought that Muslims believed they could kill and go to heaven, had been conditioned. He somehow, somewhere along the line, developed that *truth*. His mom or dad may have told him. He may have picked it up from a news story or article or an overheard conversation among peers, neighbors, or perfect strangers at the bus stop. Who knows where or how he developed his *false truth*. Regardless of how he came to believe what he did, he arrived at his opinion, the same way we all do. Fortunately, on that particular day, he got a new teacher who had an opportunity to influence his thinking, show him the real truth, and hopefully "cut a new groove" about people of the Muslim faith. We are all like the fifteen-year-old boy; full of TRUTHS from the way we've been conditioned.

The way this relates to "Getting Up When Life Blows You Down" is that your automatic reactive thoughts, *are* your *truth* about your Lifeblow. As you remember, a few of my reactive thoughts about being robbed, included, *"Poor me. Life's not fair. I've been the victim of a random act of violence. What is the world coming to? No one can be trusted."* These reactive *thoughts* were my *truth* about being shot. They were part of my belief system about anyone getting shot on their way to work while stopping at an ATM. The actual experience of being shot awakened and reinforced all of my conditioned beliefs about that happening. In other words, I already had a deep groove developed about being victimized that said, "When such a thing happens, life's not fair." That *truth* about my Lifeblow would have been awakened the same way if I had heard that you were shot on your way to work.

Each reactive thought I had about being shot represented another one of my "getting-shot/hospital-stay *truths*." A few of my reactive *truths* were, *"I have wasted the last two years of my life"* and *"I'm going to lose my job."* I had been working at my job for two years before being robbed and shot. I had spent the first year in training and most of the second year developing my territory. I had poured myself into building the business and after getting shot, felt as if the rug had been pulled out from under me. My reactive conversation was *"All my effort has gone down the tubes. The last two years of hard work, it's all been a waste. I'm going to lose my job. If that happens, I'll have to start over. What will I do then? I'm going to be married in a few months, and I really don't need this right now!"* I felt like everything I had accomplished was now lost and I felt devastated.

The longer I held these thoughts, the further down I sank in my spirits. I was absolutely certain that my past had been wasted and my future was doomed and ruined. There's not much that makes us feel worse and more depressed than when we really believe our past has been a waste, and there really is no hope for the future. My outlook created a miserable existence at my personal ground zero.

Although there was nothing wrong with any of my reactive, conditioned *truths*, they made it impossible for me to experience any fulfillment. My *truth* imprisoned me and kept me in my miserable darkness. My *truth* didn't serve me because it led to unproductive actions of beating the robber in my mind and blowing off family and friends. My *truth* didn't enable me to operate in my life at my highest potential.

The following story provides an excellent example of how we can develop *truths* that limit us in life.

Lou Tice shared the extraordinary story of a man named Cliff Young, an Australian farmer. Every year in Australia, there is a long-distance footrace from Melbourne to Sidney, a distance of 600 kilometers. This race's participants are world-class runners from around the globe.

"One particular year in the early 1990s, Cliff Young decided he would run the race. He had never run this race before and knew nothing about any of the logistics. His training consisted of chasing his cows around on the farm and performing the manual labor, required to maintain a working farm. On the day the race began, Cliff Young showed up in his 'running gear,' which consisted of a pair of overalls and galoshes. Needless to say, Cliff looked more like a man who had lost his mind and escaped from a mental institution than one who was about to compete in a 600 K race with world-class experts."

The race began with everyone holding the same opinion of Cliff Young: Here was a man who hadn't escaped from a mental facility, but ought to be in one. Making it through one day of the race would be a great showing. Completing half the race before quitting would be a phenomenal feat. Finishing the race? Well, that would be miraculous. No one could have predicted how the race actually went for Cliff the farmer.

Not only did he last more than a day, Cliff Young finished the race. Not only did he finish the race — he *won* the race. Not only did he win the race, he won the race by a day and a half! Everyone was shocked and left walking around shaking their heads in disbelief. How was this possible? Cliff certainly must have cheated somehow or misread the rules. He must have gotten off course and taken a shorter route. Upon reviewing his path, it was found that Cliff had indeed completed the race fairly, covering the entire course the same way the other runners had.

Cliff's incredible accomplishment was explained shortly thereafter when he was interviewed along with other participants. The world-class runners, when asked how to run a 600k race, all answered that you run eighteen hours and sleep six hours, then get up and do the same thing. When Cliff was interviewed about how he ran the race and won, he simply said, 'When everyone else stopped to sleep, I kept running.' When the world-class runners were told of his strategy, they thought it was nonsense. It wasn't possible for the human body to perform at optimum levels without stopping after eighteen hours and sleeping. They were the experts. They were the world-class runners. How could this guy know anything? It was difficult for them to accept that Cliff Young had kept running and won the race, simply because he "didn't know any better."

The world-class runners had their *truth* for the best way to run a 600k race. Cliff Young had another *truth* for the best way to run a 600k race. The world-class runners had a *truth*, which obviously was not the *only truth* or the *best truth*. The above story gives much insight into how we often live our lives, including in the aftermath of our Lifeblow.

Sometimes like the world-class runners, we operate in our life based on our *truth*, which is not necessarily at our highest potential. Sometimes our reactive *truth* doesn't serve us. Sometimes, because of the *truth* we hold, we aren't free to be our best in life. That's what I learned about my reactive *truth* when I was in the hospital. I learned that if I was going to be uplifted, something had to change. I would have to break out of my current belief system and find or create some new *truth* about life after being shot at an ATM. Like Cliff Young, I would have to operate out of some *new truth* in order to win my own race — a race called "Getting Up When Life Blows You Down." Operating out of *new truth*, requires *seeing new truth*, and that can be very challenging. Take a look at the sentence in the circle below.

1. What does the sentence say?
2. Now look at the above circle and sentence one more time. Once again, what does the sentence say?
3. If your answer is still A BIRD IN THE HAND, read the sentence again because that is not what it says. As you read this time, point at each word in the sentence.
4. Now, what does the sentence say?

This simple exercise is a wonderful example of how we operate after a Lifeblow. Do you notice the sentence reads "a bird in the *the* hand"? Our relationship with our Lifeblow can be like our relationship with the above sentence. We have an automatic truth about it. We are conditioned that a sentence having words put together in this particular order, says "a bird in the hand." We instantly recognize the saying and automatically, instantly, and confidently *know* that it says "a bird in the hand." That's our *truth* and we are so *right* about it, without ever realizing what we are missing. Every day of our lives, our automatic *truths* are running rampant. Some serve us and some don't. For those that don't, we can either unconsciously stick with them or look closer to see what we are missing.

Consider how unchecked truth impacted what happened on June 25, 1876. On that day, General George Armstrong Custer received information that a significant number of Indians were gathering at Little Big Horn. Without questioning his truth that he and his men could handle it, he mounted his steed and confidently rode out with two hundred fifty men to surround three thousand Indians. As the history books reflect, this was a serious mistake. General Custer's inaccurate truth proved disastrous for him and his men. Sometimes, like General Custer and the world-class runners, we run into our future, living as if our *truth* is the *only truth*. When you do that after a Lifeblow, you may not finish as a winner in the race called "Getting Up When Life Blows You Down."

Consider some more missed truths once held by people in our history.

1. "The world is flat." – People of the World

2. "Sensible and responsible women don't want to vote." – U.S. President Grover Cleveland, 1925

3. "What use could the company make of an electrical toy?"– Western Union as they rejected the rights to the telephone, 1878

4. "There is not the slightest indication that nuclear energy will ever be attainable. It would mean the atom would have to be shattered at will"– Albert Einstein, 1932

5. "Everything that can be invented, has already been." – Charles Dewell, Director, U.S. Patent Office, 1899

6. "Guitar groups are on their way out."– DECA Records, on turning down The Beatles, 1962

7. "Who the hell wants to hear actors talk?" – Harry Warner, President, Warner Brothers Studios, 1927

As ridiculous as these *truths* sound now, at the time they were spoken, they were spoken with certainty. Each of us has truths like that. After all, we are the experts on our Lifeblow. We must be careful, however, about our expert status. Like the experts who ran the 600k race, we could miss a truth or truths that make a significant and positive difference in what we get out of life. Mark Twain said, "It's not what I don't know that limits me. It's what I know that ain't so." Those words of wisdom are at the very heart of the matter of "Getting Up When Life Blows You Down."

It matters not whether our experience is one of reading a sentence that says "a bird in the the hand" or being hit with a Lifeblow. Our reactive thoughts contain *our truth*, but not necessarily *the only truth*. The ten-million-dollar question is, "If we miss the second "the" in the exercise, what else are we missing?" What are we missing in our after-Lifeblow experience that would make a significant and positive difference in how we feel and the quality of our life? What if we started to see some things we've been missing? What impact would that have on our life? Would we get more or less out of life? Would we create more or fewer possibilities for our life? The answers are all obvious. If we called into question, all of our harmful reactive truths about our Lifeblow, then discovered other positive and significant aspects to our Lifeblow, we could create NEW and better TRUTHS that enable us to "Get Up When Life Blows Us Down."

Remember my reactive *truths* that I had wasted the last two years of my life and was going to lose my job? After calling some of my customers to let them know what had happened, and explain why they weren't going to see me for a while, my customers were very complimentary and supportive, and assured me that they were going to continue doing business with us. Granted, some momentum would be lost while I was recovering, but everyone I spoke to was very understanding and told me not to worry. My Lifeblow hadn't devastated my business. I hadn't wasted the last two years of my life, but I was living into my future as if it were absolutely TRUE!

When my boss arrived at the hospital, my fears about losing my job disappeared instantly when he put his hand on my shoulder and told me the company family was behind me and not to worry about my job. He told me to take the necessary time to get well because my job would surely be waiting for me after my recovery. I'll never forget how comforting those words were. "I've wasted the last two years of my life" and "I'm going to lose my job" were simply a part of my conditioned belief system about lengthy hospital stays and recovery processes, even though they were far from true.

My conversations with my customers and boss were like seeing the second *"the"* when reading the sentence "a bird in the the hand." This information was refreshing and represented *new truth* to replace my reactionary *old truth*. The anxiety, stress, fear, and disappointment associated with my *old truths*, completely disappeared and I felt relieved and uplifted. The remainder of this book represents what I learned about discovering and creating *new truths* about Lifeblows that have the power to uplift and are therefore a springboard for "Getting Up When Life Blows You Down."

CHAPTER 6

Finding Uplifting New Meaning
after Your Lifeblow

"When I give up my need to 'Be Right' I set myself free."

A S MY REACTIVE THOUGHTS ABOUT MY SETBACK AND BEING SHOT RAN rampant, they became unfulfilling TRUTHS that lodged in my mind and took a toll on my heart. The more negative perspectives I had, the lower my spirits sank. Each negative truth created more feelings of anger, fear, frustration, discouragement, disappointment, depression, distrust, helplessness, hopelessness, self-pity, and resentment. Each negative truth added to the others. My collective perceptions led to the feelings, which led to the reactions, which led to my undesired results. My collective past *truths* made the effects of my Lifeblow bigger, more forceful, and more disastrous. I produced the same kind of result that occurs when one *bad truth* about a tailgater gets added to a bunch of other reactive *truths* and actions about a myriad of other small events. Every negative reactive truth acted like a chain that locked me down to my personal ground zero.

You are down with regard to your Lifeblow for the same reason. The longer you have been holding your negative thoughts about your challenge, the less possibility has existed for you to transform where your Lifeblow has left you. Your current thoughts are what have enabled your Lifeblow to knock you down. Your current thoughts are what have enabled your Lifeblow to keep you down. The current meaning you have brought to your challenge is the source of much to complain about. If you stopped your reactive thoughts and gave up your need to be right about truths that don't serve you, you could set yourself free to shift and alter your thinking and perspective. You could set yourself free to find new truths about your experience that you've been missing. You could replace your OLD and ONLY TRUTH with NEW, GOOD, and BETTER TRUTH, and experience a significant transformation in how your Lifeblow impacts you and your NOW moment.

While on a cruise in Alaska in 1997, I decided to go on a few excursions to see some wildlife. One of these excursions had me in a boat, on a lake with five other people. We were fairly close to the shore and one of the people spotted a bald eagle. He pointed to a tree to help everyone else see the location of this eagle. Sure enough, one by one, each person on the boat found the eagle in the tree and was enjoying the view. Everyone that is, except for me. I looked and looked and looked, trying to project a line into the tree from the end of people's fingers or standing behind them to align my eyes with their line of vision. I couldn't see the eagle. I was getting frustrated, and they started commenting on my poor eyesight. To defend myself I jokingly said, *"I think you are all crazy. There is not a bald eagle sitting in that tree. If there were, I'd easily be able to see its white head."*

When those words left my lips, five heads simultaneously spun around and out of one mouth, came the words, *"No wonder you're missing it!"* I was then informed that the object of their appreciation, the eagle, had a brown head. I looked up into the tree again and immediately saw the eagle now. Evidently, this eagle was a young eagle and the head feathers hadn't changed colors yet. For crying out loud, I had no idea that bald eagles weren't born with white heads. Every show I ever watched on Wild Discovery and every zoo I had ever visited with bald eagles on display had mature birds with white heads! All my past conditioning about bald eagles told me they <u>all</u> have white heads, all of the time. Although that was my *truth*, it certainly didn't serve me on the boat that day. My *only truth* left me feeling very frustrated and discouraged, until I became better informed and focused differently.

If I was going to experience fulfillment, I had to give up my need to be right about bald eagles having white heads. Giving up my need to be right had to come <u>before</u> I could have the fulfilling experience of watching and admiring the magnificent brown-headed bird sitting on a tree limb a short distance away. **When we give up our need to be**

right, we set ourself free to adopt a new truth and have a completely transformed experience. So it is after a Lifeblow.

I've been referring to our TRUTHS as reactive thoughts. I also like referring to them as our inner conversation — the conversation we are having with ourselves about our Lifeblow.

On the same trip to Alaska, I also decided to go on a whale-watching excursion in the Inside Passage. At one point during the day, the boat I was on stopped, and we were soon watching a humpback whale swimming a few hundred yards away. After several minutes passed, the whale began to dive. We watched its back emerge from the water a little higher than usual, followed by its tail. Fully visible above the water, its tail glistened in the sunlight before slowly disappearing under the glassy surface of the water. Our tour guide informed us that diving whales would usually stay under for nine to ten minutes before resurfacing. During the ten minutes or so that the whale was not visible, it might swim several hundred yards away or it might resurface in the same vicinity. In this particular case, the whale re-emerged fairly close to where it had last been visible to us, only this time it was swimming directly toward our boat. Initially, we thought nothing of this. Surely the whale would make a turn at some point.

I don't think anyone on the boat could have imagined what continued to unfold. The whale never diverted its path, and swam closer and closer and closer. . . . There was a hushed silence on the boat. The only noise in the midst of that beautiful scene was the sound of the whale's periodic breathing that shot a waterspout several feet into the air. Otherwise, this huge creature silently made his way toward our boat. As the whale got closer and closer, our entire perspective of this massive creature changed.

It wasn't massive. It was gigantic. No. It was enormous! I'll just say it was massively, gigantically, enormous, the biggest living thing I had ever seen in my life. The portion of its back, which was visible above the water, was four to five times as wide as our boat. The waterspout when it breathed clearly shot up fifteen to twenty feet, maybe more. As the whale got closer and closer, a part of me wondered if it was going to swim into us. As I braced myself for this possibility, I watched it breathe one final time. Then its massively gigantic and enormously humongous tail rose out of the water again, like a wall, directly in front of us. It seemed close enough to touch before disappearing in silence under our boat.

For seconds afterward, everyone was frozen and speechless. We were sitting in awe at what we had just witnessed. What was going to happen next? This was truly a magical and frightening experience. The first human sound came a few seconds later, almost by everyone on our boat simultaneously. Suddenly everyone's attention shifted away from the whale. All of us were suddenly coughing and gasping for air. We were trying to avoid breathing because we were all overwhelmed by a horrible smell. It hit everyone at the same time and everyone reacted in the same way — turning our heads away, covering our nose and mouth with our hands and arms or pulling our shirts over our faces like makeshift gas masks. Some faces turned red as people held their breath to avoid the awful smell.

The air smelled like rotten fish and it hung like a cloud over our boat. Then the questions came, "What is THAT?!," and the comments followed, *"Oh my gosh! What in the world — Gross! This is sick. Let's get out of here!"* In the background of our moans and groans, the voice of our tour guide could be faintly heard. She was giggling at our reaction and, after composing herself, informed us that what we smelled was "whale breath"! The whale had come so close to our boat that its exhaled breath, released before it dove under our boat, had settled around our boat in an invisible cloud.

Immediately after the guide informed us about the odor, my thoughts completely changed in the next few moments. I had never smelled whale breath before. I realized I might be having an experience I would never have again. With that being the case, I wanted to take full advantage of this opportunity. I immediately put my head back and took several deep breaths of fishy smelling air, savoring it as much as I would savor the aroma of freshly baked chocolate chip cookies. I took as many long deep breaths as were possible before the whale breath was gone, and you couldn't wipe the smile off my face for the rest of the day. In fact, I'm smiling now at this memory.

My experience standing on the boat and breathing that terrible smell changed dramatically in not more than the blink of an eye! My experience changed because my CONVERSATION about my experience changed. My experience changed because it took on a new

MEANING for me. My initial conversation/meaning was *"Oh man, this is sick. It smells like the waste bin in a fish factory. I want to get out of here."* After learning I was smelling whale breath, the experience took on a whole new meaning and my conversation with myself shifted to:

"Wow! This is an amazing experience. I've never smelled whale breath and probably won't ever again. This is incredible! I want to savor it and make it last. Better breathe, Bill. Better breathe deep and take it all in. Get ALL you can!"

When we start uplifting "new conversations" and create NEW TRUTH about our circumstances, fulfillment comes in an instant. There I was on a boat, standing in the middle of whale breath and nothing else had changed. My physical surroundings, the boat, our location in the water, the cloud of whale breath were all the same. The only change in how I experienced the moment was in my shift in my conversation about what was happening. Hence, the key to transforming life and "Getting Up When Life Blows You Down":

THE QUALITY OF MY LIFE EXPERIENCE HAS EVERYTHING TO DO WITH THE CONVERSATION I AM HAVING WITH MYSELF ABOUT MY LIFE EXPERIENCE.

Notice the word "everything." This truth doesn't state that "the quality of my life has "something" to do, "a little bit" to do, or "a lot" to do. . . . It states that "the quality of my life experience has EVERY-THING to do with the conversation I am having about it."

Imagine that you are at work and tomorrow will be leaving for your vacation to a tropical paradise. This day at work is a disaster. Everything is going wrong. The environment is tense. Co-workers are arguing, your boss is ranting and raving, customers are calling in upset, and a serious blame session is underway among everyone. Negativity abounds with the chaos and stress that is building up. People are snapping at each other, getting in one another's way, and complaining all the while. There you are in the midst of this horror, grinning from ear to ear while you work. Someone finally, and very sarcastically, asks you, *"What are you so happy about?"* With a sly grin, you look at your watch and calmly say, *"I'm outta here in two hours. Tomorrow — I'll be sitting on the beach."* The other person disgustedly walks away.

Notice yourself in this moment of this scenario. Everyone has a case of the sick and tireds except you. You are calm, cool, and collected. You are the most capable person at work today — to interact with an angry customer, fix a piece of equipment, handle a customer service call, and be an ideal team player in any capacity. You are "happening to life" in a most incredible way. You're happy, effective, pleasant, and productive. Life is good, as a result of the fact that the quality of your life experience has everything to do with the conversation you are having with yourself about your life experience.

Life is good because your conversation is awesome. Fast-forward now, six days into your vacation. You are lying on the beach. It's a beautiful day and you are spread out on a towel with a stomach full of lobster and a frozen drink in hand. Your eyes are closed as you soak up the breeze, the sound of waves on the shore, and the rays that warm your face and body. There's not a cloud in the sky, not a single grain of sand in your mouth. Life at this point is spectacularly great.

All of a sudden, you have a scary thought. Your eyes fly open and suddenly everything has changed. It's not that you've just been drenched by the high tide you didn't notice coming in. You're still high and dry. The grimace on your face is the result of a very uncomfortable wave of something else. All of the sudden, your mind is absorbed and consumed with dreadful thoughts — *"Oh *# ^ %*#!, Tomorrow I have to go back to work!"* Just like that, your mind has taken you back into the middle of the chaos you left a week ago. Simply put, you are sitting on a perfectly beautiful beach in the middle of paradise, MISERABLE!

The quality of your life experience has everything to do with the conversation you are having about your life experience.

You can apply this human creator or destroyer of NOW-moment fulfillment, to any Lifeblow that leaves you upset. Your Lifeblow is not what's got you down. Your inner conversation about your Lifeblow is what's got you down.

Remember my natural reactive thoughts after I was shot?

"Poor pitiful Bill. Life's not fair. I've been the victim of a random act of violence. What is the world coming to? How much time will I waste lying in the hospital? I'm going to lose my job. I can't trust anyone anymore. I've wasted the last two years of my life. I'm stupid for stopping at an ATM so early in the morning. I'm stupid for stopping when I already had money. I was minding my own business and got shot — I need to go hunt this guy down and get my revenge."

I was RIGHT about that conversation and would have argued with anyone about the truth in it. I held it with much conviction, yet my *truth* was as limiting as the truth once held that the world is flat. As long as I held it, I had no chance of experiencing fulfillment in my life. I had no chance of being my own Christopher Columbus, shattering limiting *truth* and discovering a new world for myself.

In the aftermath of any Lifeblow, there are "second *the*s" to be found and new meanings to be extracted. There are new inner conversations that have the power to uplift, encourage, and inspire you. When you start those "new conversations", you generate altered energy, feelings, and actions that enable you to get more out of life. Shifting our conversation in a way that serves us is like magnifying the positive aspects, opportunities, and possibilities. The negative aspects are still present, but it's like we've turned our "life binoculars" around and started looking at them through the side that has them appear smaller. Our focus is different and we have begun transforming our life because we can magnify the positive aspects with a new, more powerful "life telescope." We are standing tall at our personal ground zero and have begun walking out of the Lifeblow rubble, putting one foot in front of the other, upward and onward to a brighter tomorrow.

Our *old truths* won't necessarily go away. This is not a book on how to perform magic. My Lifeblow has conditioned me and still sometimes conjures up *truths* that don't serve me. For example, at nighttime or during early morning hours when it's dark and I'm not aware of anyone else being around, I have an uncontrollable sense, an automatic truth (as we defined truth earlier) that I'm in danger. It comes from my experience on September 28, 1988. On that morning, the environment was the same. It was very quiet, still and I wasn't aware of anyone else being around. My past conditioning ensures that I *know* I'm in danger and someone is about to step out of the darkness with a gun. I automatically feel afraid and anxious and want to get myself to a place where I feel safer. There may not be another human being or threat of any kind within one hundred miles; however, it is my conditioned TRUTH about dark, quiet environments when I think no one else is around. My conditioning is that "Someone is waiting for me. Someone is lurking in the darkness and wants to hurt me."

I remember one instance when I was standing outside looking up at the stars, enthralled with the beauty of the nighttime sky, and suddenly "remembered I was in danger." It was dark and quiet. I didn't have peace of mind standing outside any more, so I followed my gut feeling and went inside. I knew in the moment that my thoughts and feelings of being unsafe, were likely completely untrue. In any event, I could no longer enjoy the view because as I looked up at the stars, my conversation was "What if someone is out there and up to no good?"

I had to go. I left and traded the magnificent view of the sky for a rather humdrum view of my living room.

The quality of my life experience has everything to do with the conversation I am having about my life experience.

Although it may take awhile for OLD TRUTHS to disappear, in the meantime we can notice negative thoughts and choose to start "new conversations" to develop NEW TRUTHS that serve us. When our NEW TRUTHS cut deep enough grooves, we benefit from them. In some cases, NEW TRUTH can be assimilated into our minds to the degree that our grooves are deeper than those holding our OLD TRUTH. When that happens, our OLD TRUTH and its effects disappear.

While I am aware of what is happening with my conditioned reaction — that I might not be safe after the sun sets — I don't allow my conditioning to rule my life by never going outside after dark. My lifestyle relative to daytime/nighttime hours hasn't changed one iota, outside of when I use ATMs. I still find plenty of opportunities to look up at the stars on dark, quiet nights when I'm alone. I simply notice my reactive thoughts, understand where they are coming from and focus differently by starting a "new conversation" about living fully in the moment and reminding myself of my commitment to that. I refuse to live my life in a defensive mode to the degree that I miss out on life, particularly the beauty of the nighttime skies.

One of my favorite quotes from British playright, Tom Stoppard, is, "Words are sacred. They deserve respect. If you get the right ones, in the right order, you can nudge the world a little." What follows in this book are some ideas for putting some right words in the right order and creating some "new conversations" (*new truths*) about your after-Lifeblow now moment. These "new conversations" can nudge you out of your complaint about life and into fulfillment.

You now have an opportunity to shift your focus, stand tall, and be uplifted after your Lifeblow. These "new conversations" are not intended to be a diversion from the realities of your challenge. These "new conversations" aren't intended to discredit your thoughts and feelings. Offering these "new conversations" is not my attempt to minimize the significance of your challenge. The purpose/spirit of these "new conversations" is to uncover other areas of focus and positive significance, which can lift your spirits. John Wayne said, "Tomorrow is the most important thing in life. Comes to us at midnight — very clean. It's perfect when it arrives, and it puts itself in our hands."

These "new conversations" can be brought to any new day that puts itself in your hands. They usually aren't part of the automatic natural reactive thoughts our Lifeblows generate. Depending on the nature of your Lifeblow and how long and effectively you have been dealing with it, you may find some of the following suggested "new conversations" more helpful than others. For me, each of the "new conversations" that follow — stands alone in its effectiveness, as a powerful "life telescope" through which to look and relate to life after a Lifeblow. Collectively, they played a huge role in creating fulfillment after being robbed and shot.

Allow this new day to come to you very clean — like a blank canvas — and begin creating a masterpiece with the following new outlooks and perspectives. The following chapters cover each of the 11 Ways for "Getting Up When Life Blows You Down." At the beginning of each chapter, there is a "new conversation" that correlates to the particular perspective, or "Way To Get Up," that is covered in that chapter.

PART FOUR

**11 WAYS TO GET UP AND THRIVE
WHEN THE WINDS OF CHANGE HOWL**

CHAPTER 7

WAY #1: RE-FOCUS ON YOUR VISION
OF A BRIGHT TOMORROW

"Today is the day holding Yesterday and Tomorrow — together."

E VERY DAY, AFTER AWAKENING FROM OUR SLUMBER, WE HAVE TWO things: an ideal for what we want our life to be like and time. By the end of every day, we have created something for ourselves. Sometimes we create what we want, like and enjoy, and sometimes we do not. We've seen that one of the greatest barriers to having the life we want, is a Lifeblow. The reason Lifeblows create so much discord is because our *truth* about "how things are supposed to be" is shattered. Circumstances beyond our control aren't a part of what we have planned for any given day. When things don't turn out according to our expectations, our knee-jerk reaction is to right our wrong and fix the world (our world) so that we can be happy again.

After Lifeblows, the last place our human nature wants to look for fulfillment is within ourselves. Everything we need to stand up and walk out of our personal ground zero is already within us, patiently waiting for our pride and unhealthy reactions to sit down so we can access our confidence and power to make different choices. Getting more out of life, is only possible when we get more out of ourselves — when we become more as human beings. When the outside world changes — the faster we look in the mirror for answers, the faster we'll "Get Up When Life Blows Us Down."

There's a Chinese proverb that says, "The journey of one thousand miles begins with the first step." Beginning journeys that involve *personal change* are certainly challenging, and the journey of turning our life around after a Lifeblow is no exception. In fact, it may be one of the most difficult tasks we will ever undertake.

One of the reasons it is so important to recognize and acknowledge our reactions is because much of the time we are reacting, we are focused on the past. Why? Because we want our life to be like what it was before our Lifeblow. Our life was better then, and we want to recover our losses. What happens, however, is that while intent on the past, our focus is off other key life areas and what we want in those areas now and in the future. We often aren't aware of how our neglect and/or reactions are hurting us. If we're not careful, we lose even more than we feel our Lifeblow has already taken. That compounds our anxiety and unhappiness and leaves us feeling even more powerless. More reactions ensue and, before we know it, our life is in a downward spiral of repetitive upset, reaction, Lifeblow — upset, reaction, Lifeblow. Pulling out of this downward spiral requires that we notice what we are doing and what we are creating.

Restoring our lives requires a different focus on what we can control and create in order to experience fulfillment in the aftermath of our Lifeblow.

Helen Keller gave us a precious jewel of wisdom when she said, "Much worse than being blind would be, to be able to see, and yet have no vision." Without a clear vision of your desired future, it becomes a cinch to fall back into reactive patterns, which lead back to a life of complaint. Holding a vision of the kind of life you want is like plugging into a power source because you have connected your present situation to a brighter tomorrow. Once you see your experiences, both good and bad, as attached to a fulfilling future, you gain strength against Lifeblow reactions that persist and rob you of that future. When we hold a vision of what we want, we have tapped into a source of power, which we can draw on for sustenance. Your vision of what you want is what pulls you up, through and out of the darkness, and your "new conversation", your new message to yourself, can be:

"TODAY IS THE DAY HOLDING YESTERDAY
AND TOMORROW, TOGETHER."

This message puts the present in a new perspective — stating that without today, there is no tomorrow. Without today, and the Lifeblows and upset they bring, you have no shot at a fulfilling future. Every day we live, represents another piece of the whole we call our life. By starting this "new conversation," your focus is on having a quality life. This perspective helps you see your Lifeblow as part of a much bigger picture. Re-focusing on what you want your life to be like, after your Lifeblow, starts by asking a few simple questions:

1. What do I want my personal and professional relationships to look like?
2. What kind of health do I want in my life?
3. What do I want my business or career to look like?
4. How do I want to be spending my time to create the future I desire with regard to family, health, work, finances, and spirituality — everything I can still create in spite of my Lifeblow?

Vision provides direction and direction enables you to make choices you weren't able to make before. For example, let's imagine if you walked into a mall of 350 stores and wanted to find one particular store in five minutes.

One option would be to walk into the mall and immediately start searching for the store. You may get lucky on occasion and stumble across it quickly, but more often than not, you'll wander for a long time and probably get somewhat frustrated in the process. Remember, we're assuming you have a much more important place to be. If you wanted to avoid a frustrating search, another option would be to walk into the mall, find a directory, see where you are in proximity to the store you want to find, and make decisions about a path forward to get there as quickly as possible.

When you rediscover and focus on the things you want in the areas of life you value and cherish, and you get clear on where you are vs. where you want to be, you can move forward more productively in spite of being in the midst of very difficult circumstances. The reason is because you see a gap between CURRENT REALITY and what you WANT, and you get motivated to close the gap. You get motivated to STOP your reaction, give up your need to BE RIGHT and set yourself free to make choices that lead to your desired destination.

When I was lying in the street, moments after being shot, I experienced overwhelming feelings of fear and shock. I was focused on dying in the street. Then, there was the approaching car. As soon as I saw it, I was filled with hope. Here was the help I desperately needed. I had a vision of something I wanted, being helped, and for a moment, my pain was forgotten. You remember the car did not stop; and, as quickly as hope had entered in, it left and I was once again alone in the street.

The vision I had held moments before of a desired outcome became as distant as the tail lights on the departing car. The burning sensation in my leg returned. I couldn't move. I imagined the robber returning to "finish me off." Panic and hopelessness and helplessness consumed me once again with my expanded and more detailed focus on what I didn't want. In the next few minutes, I prepared myself to die by bringing images of my family into my mind to say goodbye. With those images, I now held a vision of something I wanted — loved ones nearby at the moment of my death. A feeling of peace consumed me.

When my will to live returned, I noticed the shadow on the sidewalk. My attention shifted to the possibility that if I could get myself into that shadow, maybe the robber wouldn't see me if he did return. The vision of myself in the shadow was one of something I wanted. Since there was a gap between current reality and what I wanted (being in the street versus protected by the shadow), that vision kicked in proactive drive and energy. Although the pain was too great to move before, I figured out a way to drag myself toward the sidewalk and comfort of the shadow. My focus on what I wanted allowed me to access the life-giving energy I needed to survive and see another tomorrow. I was attached to a brighter future. *"Today is the day holding yesterday and tomorrow together."*

Much can be learned from my moments in the street. Notice how the visions I held of things I wanted, either gave me peace, hope, strength, or inspiration at my personal ground zero. My focus on unwanted outcomes and worse case scenarios generated a completely different experience in that street — panic, hopelessness, and helplessness. Once our vision of the future we WANT becomes bigger than that which our reactive thoughts generate after a Lifeblow, we are motivated to make progress toward and create that vision.

While reacting during the first few months in the hospital, I lost focus on my vision for what I wanted my life to be like. I wanted my Lifeblow to disappear, which only caused more misery in my quest to perform the impossible. Without a compelling vision of me and my family and friends taking advantage of <u>every</u> opportunity of being together (including times I might be in a hospital), it was impossible for me to break out of my sabotaging thoughts and behavior. I went on shutting people out of my life and creating a life worth complaining about.

As I strengthened my vision of loving, caring, supportive, and attentive relationships with family and friends, it became easier to make adjustments in my reactive thinking and behaving. The magic of an internalized and focused vision is that it works on us from the inside out (versus our Lifeblow working on us from the outside-in). With our vision of what we want, we are *happening to life*. My vision of what I wanted provided a firm foundation where I could anchor myself and make better decisions about how I spent my time. As a result of focusing on what I wanted my relationships to be like, I stopped pulling away from friends and family. I became more welcoming, attentive, and appreciative of important people in my life. When we focus on a compelling vision, we create a new reality for ourselves. Antoine de Saint-Exupery put it this way: "A rock pile ceases to be a rock pile the moment a single man contemplates it, bearing within him the image of a cathedral."

The firemen and rescue workers in the hours and days after the terrorist attacks applied that wisdom while in the midst of their shock, disbelief, and chaos. They watched with horror as planes crashed into buildings, people jumped to their death, and skyscrapers collapsed. They knew thousands of people were inside, trapped, and probably killed, including many of their own. How in the world did surviving firefighters and rescue workers regroup so quickly and begin picking rubble up by the handfuls to put in five-gallon buckets? How did they not only do that, but continue that effort day and night, day after day after day? How would you have done it?

We've all seen the picture of the three firemen raising the American flag in the midst of the rubble that used to be the World Trade Center. That was done the day after the attacks, on September 12, at Ground Zero. Then we saw the images on TV of the huge

American flag being unfurled by firemen off the roof of the Pentagon. Those flags symbolized America and all that America stands for and all that America represents — FREE, PROGRESSIVE, STRONG, AND SAFE. The firemen and rescue workers were able to work through exhaustion, day and night, because they had something to look to and focus on. When they saw red, white, and blue, they held a vision of a free and safe America, and it sustained them and spurred them on. They worked while holding the "new conversation": *"Today is the day holding yesterday and tomorrow together."*

While watching the news on the morning of October 15, 2001, I heard a story that demonstrates how important, uplifting, and energizing it is to stay focused on a compelling vision of the future. The Empire State Building had been illuminated red, white, and blue, each night since the attacks. On October 14, these lights were turned off. When the firefighters and rescue workers showed up to work that night, and didn't see the lights, they demanded the lights be turned back on. They needed to be able to see the American colors and draw continued strength and purpose to square their shoulders, lift their heads, and stand tall at Ground Zero, doing whatever would be necessary to restore America. If that included picking up tons and tons of rubble by the handfuls, so be it. In order to experience a bright and fulfilling future, we too must "keep the lights turned on," illuminate our vision, and stay focused on a bright tomorrow.

When you think about the person you want to be, and what you want to create your relationships and life to be, you can make your personal ground zero experience a part of your journey, instead of a misstep into a deep, dark chasm where fulfilling futures disappear. Holding a vision of a bright future has a positive impact on your Lifeblow reactions instead of your Lifeblow reactions having a negative impact on your future. Personal ground zeros can be transformed from disastrous to a disaster to be dealt with, when we view them as being attached to, and therefore a part of, our journey toward a brighter tomorrow. Fulfillment isn't possible by trying to change the past. Fulfillment comes by creating worthwhile Now moments and living into bright futures. Holding a compelling vision makes that possible. Raise your flag and focus on the vision of what you want, and can cause your life to be like. Get underway with the "new conversation": *"Today is the day holding yesterday and tomorrow together."*

ASK YOURSELF:

Relative to my key life areas of Health, Financial, Business/Career, Spirituality, Family, Personal & Professional Relationships, and Recreation:

1. What have I always wanted in these areas?

2. What am I committed to create in these areas?

3. If I "had it all" in these areas, what would my life look like?

4. What have I always wanted to be, do, have, experience, and share in these areas?

5. What can I restore that my Lifeblow reactions have damaged?

* *Note: These answers are focused on what you can still create, have, and enjoy.*

CHAPTER 8

WAY #2: KNOW WHY YOU WAKE UP IN THE MORNING

"When my "WHY" is big enough, I'll figure out HOW."

WHAT'S MISSING IN OUR STRUGGLE TO HAVE FULFILLMENT IS NOT only a compelling enough vision of what we WANT, but also clarity on WHY we want it, WHY we value it, and WHY it's worth our effort. Our WHY is our purpose, and it awakens commitment, dedication, and our sense of self, giving us more energy, strength and resilience. The new life energy we gain by having purpose reinforcing our desires (vision of what we want), enables us to have more resilience at our personal ground zero.

Imagine hiking up a mountain through a forest to find a waterfall. You venture out and progress seems easy, but then you encounter your first obstacle. It's a fallen tree. You struggle over it, bumping your knee and falling hard to the ground on the other side. You pick yourself up, groaning with pain, and continue on. Soon afterward, it begins to rain and the next barrier appears in the form of a low, overhanging branch. You crawl under it, but stand up too quickly on the slippery slope and bang your head regaining your balance. A knot forms immediately, and your head starts to pound. You limp on in pain and a few minutes later the rain stops. That's good, but the bugs that come out, are not. They are biting every exposed part of your body. You continuously swat at these tiny monsters, but they just keep biting and biting and biting. . . .

It doesn't take long to realize that along the entire hike, there will be more fallen trees, stumps, overhanging branches, high ledges, ravines, snakes, quicksand and lions and tigers and bears. . . . Oh my! No one said it would be like this! You're hardly into your journey and already feeling the effects of blisters, burning muscles, and trickling blood. The sweltering heat creates rashes and sweat beads that sting your eyes. You are the walking wounded. Suddenly, you notice that your thoughts sound like familiar words you've heard or said on the way to Disney World, "When are we going to be there?" After a few more bites, slips, and bumps, you decide that turning around is a much better option. It's just not worth it. This trek is way too uncomfortable and not any fun; in fact, it's downright miserable. Time to head back to the car.

Your journey of creating fulfillment after a Lifeblow can be a lot like that. All this uncomfortable business of giving up your need to be right and shifting your thinking. For crying out loud, it's so much easier just being your reactive self and staying the same. That's why your subconscious mind screams at you: "GO BACK WHERE YOU BELONG!" A game of tug-of-war is being played between your ears. Your higher self is making headway and your reactive self is dug in and putting up one heck of a fight to keep you there. Too often, we turn back and throw in the towel on becoming more, and never give ourselves a chance to be victorious over our Lifeblow.

When your "hike" becomes uncomfortable, dreadful, painful, agonizing, and exhausting, it isn't the lump on your head or the bug bites that keep you going. It's not the trickling blood that inspires you to take another step. It's not your reactive conversations that will keep you going when the chips are down and things get downright miserable.

The thing that enables you to keep looking up, going up, and "gutting it out" toward what you want, is being clear on WHY you want to reach the waterfall, WHY it's worth staying in the fight, and WHY you value the experience. Dag Hammarskjold, in *Markings*, said, "When morning's freshness has been replaced by the weariness of mid-day, when the leg muscles quiver under the strain, the climb seems endless, and suddenly, nothing will go quite as you wish — it is then that you must not hesitate." Many people give up their pursuit of the life they want, just before realizing the reward of their effort. If they only stayed focused on their desire and the purpose of their actions, they would realize the joy and fulfillment that awaits the next step.

When you are hiking up a mountain, tired, bruised, and fed up, but keep going anyway with a smile on your face, you're not after water falling off a rock ledge. You're after the splendid beauty of it. You're after the miraculous view of the planet from way up there. You're after what a fried chicken picnic tastes like on top of the world. You're after the rush you get standing at its edge, hearing it roar and feeling the cool mist soothe your battered body.

You're after the feelings that accompany your look of awe at perfect beauty. You're after sitting quietly under the heavens and feeling God's presence. You're after the refreshing dive into the crystal clear water at the bottom of the falls. You're after the exhilaration of careening over the edge in a fifty-five-gallon barrel, and the priceless look on your spouse's face as you free-fall 500 feet. Okay, so I'm getting a bit carried away, but hopefully you get the point. *You're after the reward and benefit this experience brings you!* Focusing on that instead of the bug bites and aching body enables you stay the course and find fulfillment on the other side of your mountainous challenge, knowing that if you made it here, you can make it anywhere. That's the wisdom behind the "new conversation":

WHEN MY WHY IS BIG ENOUGH, I'LL FIGURE OUT HOW.

I've had people ask me, "How in the world did you stay confined to the same bed for three months without moving around? There's no way I could have done that." Whenever that was said to me, I would always tell the person that my WHY for staying still in bed, made it very easy. If I didn't, my leg wouldn't heal properly. I would lose the progress of being in traction thus far and prolong the healing process. I was also told of the risk of one leg ending up shorter than the other, which could result in future complications with my back. If I wanted to eliminate those risks and walk normally again, I wanted to stay still in bed. Even though I was acting like an idiot some of the time, part of me was smart enough to know that I had a choice between dealing with bedsores for another few months or dealing with possible chronic pain for several years. Given my options, it was easy to lie there patiently and do my time. *"When my why is big enough, I'll figure out how."*

Benjamin Disraeli said, "The secret of success is constancy to purpose." When you are focused on what you do by being clear about WHY you do it, you can accomplish things you otherwise couldn't. Like vision, purpose not only gives us resilience, but it also gives us new energy to do what it takes to achieve desired outcomes.

A man was walking home from work one evening. He was running a bit late, so decided to take a shortcut through a cemetery. It was getting dark and difficult to see, and the man never saw the freshly dug grave in front of him. A split second later, he was lying in the bottom of it. Fortunately he wasn't hurt, so he collected himself and spent the next thirty minutes trying to climb out. The walls were steep and very slippery, so all his efforts were to no avail. Exhausted, he crouched at one end of the grave and decided he would try to get some sleep while waiting for morning to arrive, when he would call out for help to someone visiting or working there the next day.

Just as he was dozing off, he was awakened by a thud, followed by groans from another person. Someone else walking along had just fallen into the same grave! The first man didn't say a word, but just watched as this second person rose, dusted himself off and then tried to get out. An hour passed and the second guy hadn't come close to scaling the wall of the grave. The first man, hidden in the shadows, was getting frustrated just watching this effort and finally couldn't help himself. Just as the second man was about to give up, the first guy walked to the other end of the grave, touched him on the shoulder, and said, "You are never going to get out of here." Before all those words were out of his mouth, the second guy shot out of that grave like a rocket!

This story illustrates what is possible in the aftermath of a Lifeblow, where we're left feeling like we're in a dark, deep pit with no way out. Unless we are emotionally attached to a compelling vision and sense of purpose, the motions we go through aren't worth the effort. Purpose enables you to keep on keeping on, because you know how incredibly worthwhile your effort is. With a strong sense of purpose, more new life energy is ignited. Like the man who shot out of the grave, we can accomplish what we couldn't before. Your vision gives you drive and direction. **Your purpose taps into afterburner resources you didn't know you had.** You find new energy to scale the steep walls in the dark hole called your personal ground zero. It doesn't have to become your grave. That's the magic in the "new conversation": *"When my why is big enough, I'll figure out how."*

After the terrorist attacks, a newscaster was talking to a city official and said, "People working close to Ground Zero will walk through debris and into their office buildings on Monday, 9/17. They will go up dozens of floors, look out their windows where they would normally see the twin towers, be reminded of what happened, but sit behind their desks anyway and resume work. That is remarkable."

The official's answer was, "Yes, it is remarkable, and they will do it day after day until the rubble is gone and the city is rebuilt."

All I could think about was the sense of purpose driving these people to return to work. All workers had a purpose to provide for themselves and their families. They had a purpose to reach professional goals they had set. People had purposes to fulfill promises that had been made to customers, associates, coworkers, and employers. In addition, there was a purpose to show the terrorists that their actions could never stop the American spirit, that we are strong and resilient, and our lives would not shut down. Purpose has the power to lead people to make choices that override reactionary thinking. With the power of purpose working in our lives, staying home and doing nothing isn't much of an option. *"When my why is big enough, I'll figure out how."*

That same purposeful strength can be seen in the example of a fireman working at Ground Zero, who said he talked to his wife on the afternoon of 9/11 and knew his family was safe, but actually didn't make it home for three days. He described what it was like when his wife met him at the door. He said, "She never looked so beautiful and precious before." He gave her a hug and they held each other, and held each other some more. Then he went upstairs to see his kids. He touched them, held them, kissed them, and returned downstairs. Anyone would understand if he had stayed at home, prolonged his hugs, and collapsed into bed.

That didn't happen to the fireman who woke up that morning with a purpose to save lives. He didn't sit down — he couldn't. When his wife asked what was wrong, he walked over to her and said, "Now that I've been home and seen you, seen for myself that all of you are okay , I've got to go back."

When his wife asked why, he replied, "Because the rest of my family is still down there." Although exhausted, his purpose was wide awake, his afterburner resources were tapped, and he walked out the front door, returned to Ground Zero, and resumed looking for the rest of his family.

At one stage while I was in the hospital, and as a result of being confined in traction and not moving around much, I developed a blood clot in my lung. I was rushed downstairs and one of the nurses, who helped give me a CT scan, asked me if I remembered her. I did not and she then informed me that she had been in the emergency room when I was wheeled in after being shot. She asked me if I really knew how lucky I was to be alive.

This nurse then told me that some people die when they get a blood clot in their lung. Smiling down at me before I was wheeled back to my room, she grabbed my hand and told me, "Count your blessings. Twice now, you are very, very fortunate."

Oh, how I wish I could thank that nurse today. She illuminated that day and many others with her perspective and wonderful reminder that we really never know what might happen at any given moment on any given day. We could be here one minute and gone the next. That's a great purpose for stopping unhealthy reactions that lead to unfulfilled lives. Peter Drucker said "Destiny is a lot like attitude. It's not a matter of chance. It's a matter of choice." One way to choose wisely in the aftermath of your Lifeblow is to take full advantage of another chance to enjoy the company of family and friends. When you bring that kind of purpose to each new day, you'll realize the power in the "new conversation": *"When my why is big enough, I'll figure out how."*

ASK YOURSELF:

1. For all the wants and desires I identified at the end of Chapter 7, WHY do I want them?

2. WHY am I committed to those things?

3. WHY would I go through any effort to create that vision for myself?

4. What purpose do I have for still being alive?

5. Who needs me as a productive and capable person to look to as an example?

CHAPTER 9

WAY #3: ACCEPT RESPONSIBILITY FOR GROWING FROM YOUR LIFEBLOW

"All challenges and setbacks give me a tremendous personal advantage."

EVERY LIFEBLOW IS AN OPPORTUNITY IN DISGUISE TO GROW AS A human being. We've all heard the saying, "That which doesn't kill me, only makes me stronger." Every Lifeblow holds the opportunity for becoming more by becoming stronger. In fact, the greater our Lifeblow, the greater our opportunity for growth. This entire book represents how I've grown after being shot. I've grown in my awareness of the costs of my reactions and my ability to stop them and respond with "new conversations." My experience helped me build on and develop character qualities such as self-control, patience, flexibility, a sense of humor, understanding, gratitude, grace under pressure, and the ability to forgive. These enable me to stay in a responsive mode, more often, when faced with challenges that arise each day. I handle Lifeblows more effectively than I used to, which helps me stay on track with creating more of the life I want.

It is clear to me that the areas of growth, made possible by being shot, are truly priceless to me for the difference they make in my life today. Even with a trillion dollars, there is not a store in the world where I could buy gifts like self-control, gratitude, patience, and understanding. One of the biggest gifts of being shot is how I grew from that experience. I learned that with each challenging change we face, there is an opportunity to re-invent ourselves as more capable human beings — and have a better life in the process. That's how I learned the "new conversation":

ALL CHALLENGES AND SETBACKS GIVE ME
A TREMENDOUS PERSONAL ADVANTAGE.

Jim Rohn said, "Let life touch you. Reach into the past for something valuable, called experience. Don't get *through* the day. Get *from* the day."

Let life touch you by allowing life to *teach* you. Take from your experience lessons and insights that make a difference in your future, both by applying them yourself and sharing them with others. Learning requires that we accept responsibility for our Lifeblow. Initially, this idea may sound crazy to you. Some Lifeblows are brought about by circumstances that seem out of our control; however, sometimes there are ways we contributed to our Lifeblow with our decisions and choices.

When we discover some of those, we can use them to prevent our creation of future Lifeblows and experience a sense of fulfillment and confidence going forward. Learning and applying lessons to create a brighter tomorrow is another way to "Get Up When Life Blows You Down."

Sometimes it can be helpful to have a mentor or life coach to help and challenge us to make progress after a Lifeblow. I provide that service, as do many others, and the following is an example of an insight I gleaned from such a person. When my coach first invited me to accept one hundred percent responsibility for being robbed and shot, I told the guy he was nuts. There was no way I was responsible when I was minding my own business on my way to work and I was RIGHT about that. Yet, in time I was able to make progress with this idea when my mentor told me that "accepting responsibility for being shot," didn't mean I was actually responsible. He told me to pretend that I was responsible. He told me to simply hold the thought — to take this responsibility attitude and "try it on," like I would try on a jacket I didn't own. I didn't have to "buy it," just try it on and take a look at myself and my experience from that perspective. In other words, pretend I was responsible and look for things I could have done differently.

My coach told me that the easiest way to do that is to treat the process like playing a game. Call the game "Accepting Responsibility for My Lifeblow," instead of "Monopoly." Just like you pretend you bought Park Place and purchased a hotel, pretend you are completely responsible for your Lifeblow. It will be critical to treat this process like a game, so you do not allow this process to backfire. You want to be careful to not start a blame session, where you start beating yourself up for what happened. I once made that mistake, as I will share in the following chapter. This responsibility conversation is to be applied to make a positive difference now and in the future, not leave you feeling worse about the past and stuck at your personal ground zero.

Begin the game by asking, "Okay, if I'm responsible for my Lifeblow, if I contributed to it, what could I have done differently?" Now simply answer that question, in as many ways you can. Let your imagination soar. The answers won't all be practical. That's okay. The point is that in some answers to that question, there may be an insight that can serve you now and in the future. It's possible you won't have any answers. There may have been nothing you would have done differently. Some answers may come later in your process.

My answers to the above question included the following:

- *I could have been involved in the design of ATMs to make users less vulnerable.*
- *I could have not stopped at the ATM at 4:30 AM.*
- *I could have waited until daylight and used a different machine in another town.*
- *I could have driven around the bank and possibly seen the robber before jumping out of my car.*
- *I could have used an ATM where there were more people around.*
- *I could have avoided using an ATM at all.*
- *Perhaps if I had been able to not react, by seeing the robber differently and sending love, there would have been a different outcome.*
- *I could have been volunteering my time as a Big Brother or working with kids at risk, serving as a positive role model. If I had done that, maybe I would have crossed paths with this robber when he was younger. Perhaps I could have been a positive role model in a way that would have made a positive difference in his choices and resulting path in life.*

As you can see from my answers, some were more practical than the others. That's okay. In playing the game, we're not trying to be practical. Our objective is to pull ourselves out of our victim mindset where we have no power, control, or ability to create a fulfilling now moment and future. After we come up with every conceivable answer, no matter how farfetched they seem — we can call "Game over." It's the process of playing that might produce a breakthrough thought that pays off big. In chapter 16, titled "Selflessly Give and Abundantly Receive," I will share how the seemingly "impractical" answer that, *"I could have been volunteering my time with kids at risk. Had I done that, it's possible that I could have been a positive role model for the robber in a way that would have made a difference in his choices and resulting path in life,"* also contributed greatly to my experiencing fulfillment after being shot. For now, I'll simply share how the practical answers helped me "Get Up When Life Blew Me Down."

One very simple lesson that I learned from my Lifeblow is to stop using ATMs when it's dark, particularly during pre-dawn hours. I still use ATMs today. Like the motivation we have for not allowing terrorists to take our freedoms and "shut down" our lives, I have that purpose with regard to using ATMs. I find ATMs to be very convenient. My gift is that I have an awareness I didn't have before, when I do use them. If I am alone, I drive around the building first to notice if anyone else is nearby. What I do from there depends on what/who I see and what my instincts tell me to do. I now know how easy a target I am, so I use ATMs less frequently. When I do use them, it's usually during daylight hours and at locations where there are many other people around, such as grocery stores.

These may sound obvious to you. You may already follow such guidelines when you use ATMs; however, for me they were major shifts from when and where I was using them before — when I thought my truth was that nothing would ever happen to me. After seeing the robber, I accepted a new truth that it could happen. Then, I reacted out of that new thought, which resulted in my vulnerability. Vernon Law said, "Experience is a hard teacher because she gives us the test first, the lesson afterwards." Our responsibility is to gratefully find and accept the lessons and then apply them.

After accepting responsibility for how I contributed to my

Lifeblow, I reminded myself that we do create our lives by choice. I drove myself to the ATM. I was responsible for being there and not seeing the robber. I accepted responsibility for my reaction and how I became vulnerable. This acceptance of responsibility, led to an enlightened conversation: "If I created one thing, I can certainly create something else and it can be a better something else." I learned how to avoid a repeat. In that way, being shot has definitely served me. *"All challenges and setbacks give me a tremendous personal advantage."*

It is believed that the terrorist attacks, succeeded more easily because of a situation in France a few years before. There, terrorists hijacked a plane and wanted the pilots to fly it into the Eiffel Tower. The pilots said they had to refuel and upon landing, the plane was stormed and the terrorists arrested. This is believed to have been when the terrorists decided they had to learn how to fly planes. For crying out loud, if terrorists are accepting responsibility for their mistakes and setbacks, we had better accept responsibility for our own.

Security in our country has improved dramatically since the terrorist attacks. Travel on commercial airlines is safer than it ever has been. Airport and airline security will never, ever be the same. It will be bolstered and updated and improved. Efforts are underway to replace and strengthen cockpit doors, as well as to have marshals as part of the flight crew on flights.

Governments of the entire free world accepted responsibility for the terrorist attacks by acknowledging that they could have been working together better, sharing intelligence and resources which will make it more difficult for terrorist groups to operate in the future. President Bush accepted responsibility for the attacks by creating a new cabinet position, the Office of Homeland Security to pursue terrorism, defend America from future attacks, and preserve our freedom. As a result of all these changes brought about by lessons learned, more terrorists will be caught and more attacks thwarted. *"All challenges and setbacks give me a tremendous personal advantage."*

Stanislaw Jerzy Lee in *More Unkempt Thoughts* said, "No snowflake in an avalanche ever feels responsible." Wherever we go, there we are as human beings making choices – consciously or unconsciously. The common thread running through every facet of what each of us calls "my life", is our individual presence there. Our individual world is like a pile of snow and each of us is like a snowflake in that world. Our mere existence in our life contributes to our outcomes (by what we choose to do or by what we choose to leave undone), but we often don't accept responsibility for our part. When that's the case, we do others and ourselves a great disservice.

Allow the memories of the passengers aboard United Airlines flight 93, the jet that crashed south of Pittsburgh on the morning of 9/11, to inspire you to accept responsibility for your circumstances. The forty-five people on board at the time of the hijacking, saw their personal ground zero in an airplane hanging in the sky at 10,000 feet, and accepted responsibility for what was happening. Passengers fought back and thwarted the terrorists' mission, saving untold lives when that plane never made it to its intended target.

By the end of the week, their heroic actions inspired this responsibility attitude in pilots and passengers aboard one of the first regular flights after the attack. The pilot reportedly made an announcement to his passengers, "We are 200 people and any would be terrorists on this flight are severely outnumbered." He reminded his passengers that they could do what passengers on flight 93 had done. He encouraged them to be proactive, to accept responsibility. Imagine the resistance those terrorists would face if they attempted to do the same thing today.

Your Lifeblow holds lessons and insights that you can learn and apply to make a positive difference in your future. Winston Churchill said, "Men and women occasionally stumble over the truth, but most of them hurry off as if nothing happened." Many people would learn from their mistakes if they weren't so busy denying they made them. Don't make that mistake. The only thing more painful than learning from experience is not learning from experience. Let life teach you.

Once you know that every challenge contains precious jewels of wisdom, Lifeblows can be seen as gateways to a more fulfilling life, sometimes in ways we may have never thought of. **Life doesn't have to be measured <u>only</u> by what Lifeblows take from you. Life can also be measured by what you gain and how you grow from Lifeblows.** It's not possible to grow, gain and remain at your personal ground zero. Start the "new conversation": *"All challenges and setbacks give me a tremendous personal advantage."*

ASK YOURSELF:

1. How is my Lifeblow an opportunity to be more patient, kind, faithful, caring, loving, and supportive?

2. How is my challenge an opportunity to be more, do more, have more, experience more, and share more in my life?

3. What lessons can I learn from my setback that will make a positive difference in my future and add value to my life experience?

4. What lessons can I learn and share with others?

5. Where can I accept responsibility for my Lifeblow (where I haven't been) and be inspired by what that makes possible in my future?

CHAPTER 10

WAY #4: GIVE YOURSELF CREDIT FOR BEING VALUABLE

"What you think of me is none of my business."

*I*N THE AFTERMATH OF YOUR LIFEBLOW, depending on the nature of it, part of your struggle can be with yourself. We often blame ourselves for what happened and start punishing conversations about how idiotic we are. As discussed in the last chapter, accepting responsibility for how we contributed to our Lifeblow, is a very worthwhile process. Valuable lessons can be learned and applied to the future to create more fulfillment. However, there is a fine line between learning lessons from our past and beating ourselves up over it. There's not much we can do to ourselves that is more damaging over the long haul than beating ourselves up because we "should have known better."

I've done some things in my life where I've kicked myself afterward because I inherently knew I might regret my actions while I was in mid-stride of doing them. Peer pressure, seeking acceptance, going along with the crowd, wanting to fit in, feeling the need to be in control — are all weaknesses that often steamroll over our higher consciousness. When that's the case, we're going to be upset with ourselves for what we might call a stupid mistake. Such instances become opportunities to develop more self-control and grow in our ability to honor our deepest truth for having the life we want. From that standpoint, "I should have known better" is a reactive conversation that is healthy over the short haul because it gets us back on track.

In other cases, some of our Lifeblows might be repeats from the past. It is very difficult to NOT beat ourselves up when we can see that we have repeated the same mistake more than once. Sophia Loren said, "Mistakes are a part of the dues one pays for a full life." "I should have known better" can be a <u>short-term</u> conversation that has us get serious about accepting responsibility for growing from our Lifeblow.

In some cases we beat ourselves up because, in looking back at our Lifeblow, it is obvious that we could have done a few things differently and avoided disaster or unwanted results.

Regardless of *why* we beat ourselves up, and separate from whether or not that activity helps us get back on track, remember that over the long haul, beating yourself up will lead you away from the fulfillment you seek. We can beat ourselves down to the point where we lose part of ourselves by lowering our self-esteem and self-image, unable to have a fulfilling experience in our day-to-day life.

When we tell ourselves we are stupid and wrong, over and over, the result is no different than the damage that is done when another person repeatedly sends us that message. In the work I have done with women of every ethnic background and class who have been battered and abused, we talk a lot about the importance of self-esteem and how to nurture it. One way is by NOT buying into the criticism and demeaning things that are said to us. Another person's words can tear down and destroy a part of us, ONLY when we accept what they say as our truth about ourselves. Just because someone else has an opinion that I'm a loser, doesn't make me a loser. I become a loser when <u>their opinion</u> turns into <u>my belief</u> about myself. Eleanor Roosevelt said it this way, "No one can make you feel inferior without your consent."

The more we internalize another person's opinions, the more we believe them. The more we believe them, the more evidence we find in every aspect of life to support that opinion. If I see myself as valuable, I will gather evidence to prove to myself that I am valuable. By the same token, if I see myself as stupid, I will see all sorts of evidence to show I'm stupid and continue to whittle away at my confidence and self-respect. Rising out of your personal ground zero requires that you stop holding negative and critical beliefs about yourself, whether they are self started or the opinions of others. You do that when you start the "new conversation:"

WHAT YOU THINK OF ME IS NONE OF MY BUSINESS.

After my experience of being shot, I found myself buying into negative messages. My conversation was:

> *"I'm such an idiot for stopping at an ATM at 4:30 AM. I'm so stupid for not only stopping at that hour, but also for being at the ATM with $60 in my pocket! I should have known better! I put myself into a position to be shot."*

I felt embarrassed, ashamed, and bad about myself. Each time I said those words, I dug my hole a little deeper.

In addition to criticizing myself, the same demeaning message of being stupid was sometimes expressed and reinforced by other people. After learning that I was using an ATM at 4:30 AM, many people view my action as poor judgment. People have been quick to express their opinion that being at an ATM so early, was really, really dumb. Even today, many years after the shooting, I still get that opinion on occasion. On an evaluation form, filled out after a speech I gave several years after the shooting, one lady wrote, "If you were stupid enough to be at an ATM at 4:30 AM, you deserved to be shot."

I remember reading that evaluation and sinking inside. All of a sudden, I felt horrible about myself. Before even realizing it, I had drifted back into my reactive thoughts about myself when I was in the hospital. "Maybe she's right. Maybe I was stupid." Then I added to my battery against myself by thinking, "If this is what my message brings out in people, if this is the impact I have, I need to find something else to do." Five minutes into beating myself up and wondering what I should do next for a living, I noticed the stack of remaining evaluations. I picked them up and one by one, started reading.

When I was through, I decided to continue as a professional speaker. I caught myself allowing negative opinions of one person, to become part of my thinking about myself. We must be careful not to allow ourselves to be dragged down by negative opinions of others. Since there was nothing I could take away from her comments to improve my presentation, before leaving the post office I dropped the first evaluation in the trash. As it fell into the bin, I silently said to my reactionary self AND the woman who wrote the evaluation: *"What you think of me is none of my business."*

The next time someone criticizes or belittles you, consider looking at them with a smile on your face and saying, "Thank you for sharing, but what you think of me is none of my business." Be calm and considerate. Inform them like you would inform them that a rainstorm is coming. When those words leave your lips, you will likely observe a perplexed look. My experience shows that they may even be speechless, as they think about what you just said, what it means, and how they can be that kind of stand for themselves.

Even if you choose not to say those words out loud, saying them silently is also very powerful. You are consciously aware that you are guarding yourself from having negative words and opinions enter your mind and become a part of you and the life you create. Although negative opinions of others will always be out there, they are never an excuse for missing out on fulfillment. Each of us can ultimately choose what we allow to take on as beliefs about ourselves, and our circumstances.

Creating fulfillment today and tomorrow isn't possible when you beat yourself up about the past. It's easy to look back and say, "I should've done this or that," but the reality is *we were different people before our Lifeblow*. We were different because our awareness was different. Most of the time, each of us is doing our best in any given moment with the information we have.

I was doing that on the morning of 9/28/88 — using an ATM I had used many times before without incident. You were doing that when your Lifeblow hit. You were living your life based on the attitudes and beliefs you developed from all of your past experiences. At the time of your Lifeblow, you didn't have the awareness, attitudes, and beliefs that you gained <u>after</u> your Lifeblow. **You are being unfair to yourself when you use insights you gain from looking back, to beat yourself up for what happened before you had them.**

The quality of my life experience changed dramatically in the hospital when I stopped beating myself up and started taking credit for being valuable. My responsive self-talk became:

"I was up at 4:30 AM because I have a good work ethic and was on my way to work to serve other human beings. I stopped to use the ATM even though I had money in my pocket, because I knew I would need more cash by the end of the day. I was planning ahead;, not a bad quality to have in business and life."

Each of these perspectives was true and just as available as "I'm stupid."

Our words have incredible power. They have the power to uplift and inspire or tear down and destroy. No new perspective is small when it creates an uplifted state. As is the case for all new and uplifting conversations, they create an opening to make other attitude shifts and start more "new conversations." Each "new conversation" and its benefit opened room for the next and the next. That opened up the possibility for every day to hold new awareness and perspective shifts to create a more fulfilling and promising future. When we stop beating ourselves up and make adjustments in our internal conversation to give ourselves credit for being valuable, we've started loving ourselves again. That's the best reason of all to start the "new conversation": *"What you think of me is none of my business."*

Women in Afghanistan have shown us what is possible in the midst of negativity and oppression. After the Taliban took power in 1996, the women of Afghanistan were not allowed to work or go out in public by themselves, unless escorted by a male relative. Girls over eight years of age were not allowed to go to school. After the Taliban took control, professional women such as professors, doctors, lawyers, artists, and writers were forced from their jobs and restricted to their homes, where they had to stay inside, like prisoners, behind walls and windows that had been painted to prevent sunlight from penetrating. Because they weren't allowed to work, many were starving.

Parueen Hashafi, an Afghan woman radio announcer before the Taliban took control, described her life as a single, jobless woman with a monotonous routine of waking, eating, cleaning, and sleeping. She said, "Under Taliban rule we were neither alive or dead."

Another Afghan woman echoed her thoughts after Kabul was freed, when she described a woman's life under Taliban rule, "It was like we were in prison. We had no life. There was nothing for us to do. We were not people."

The basic message being sent to the women of Afghanistan, day in and day out, had been "You are stupid, worthless, and no good." Every day they woke up, began a new day full of fear, disrespect, and oppression, with the possibility of being beaten, stoned, tortured, or killed. Their lives on a day-to-day basis was unimaginable to us in the free world, yet there were some women in Afghanistan who refused to fully conform and allow such demeaning and limiting messages to become a part of their thinking. Instead of buying in to those opinions of themselves or holding thoughts that they couldn't overcome their circumstances, some women started a "new conversation": *"What you think of me is none of my business."*

Perhaps you saw the Afghan woman who secretly escaped Afghanistan and made it to New York to do an interview on US television. She spoke of her involvement with an underground group of women living in Afghanistan and numbering a few thousand. She said they were organized and committed to speaking out about their oppression, raising awareness in the world for their horrific conditions, and never fully conforming to the opinions of the Taliban.

Pictures had been taken of members of this group, not wearing burquas. While in public, they wore lipstick and makeup underneath their burquas, maintaining their freedom to choose and keeping their self-respect in tact. Although it was very risky, no one was going to take away their freedom to choose. They refused to let go of memories of a time less than a decade ago, when they wore clothing of choice and attended universities to learn, grow, and become more. If these women were going to die, they were going to do so with their sense of self and self-respect in tact. Memories of a brighter past had been turned into a vision of a brighter future and a source of strength to prevail in such horrid conditions.

Instead of living a life confined to waking, eating, cleaning, and sleeping, these women were choosing to live for a worthy ideal, in spite of Taliban rule. In what otherwise was a treacherous, hostile, brutal, and potentially deathly environment, they found fulfillment in the "new conversation": *"What you think of me is none of my business."*

From the time the Taliban took control, they oppressed not only women, but also men. Afghan men were forced to grow their beards to a prescribed length. The Taliban had empowered street enforcers to whip men into Mosques to pray. After the fall of Kabul to US Marines in November of 2001, men exultantly shaved off their beards for the first time in years. Ahmad Rashef had his beard cut for the first time in five years, saying, "Being shaved is like being free."

Before Kabul fell, music had been banned completely; however, on November 14, audiocassette recorders were taken out and men and women played music in public. Abdul Rehmen, blared his favorite cassette in the street at full volume. He spoke of how he, like the women I mentioned earlier, had preserved his sense of self and self-respect during Taliban rule. Abdul said, "I used to play this at home very quietly, always checking to see if anyone was outside." This was his way of making his personal Declaration of Independence.

Finding fulfillment after a Lifeblow requires making a personal Declaration of Independence, to live independently from the negative influence of other people and your reactive negative thoughts. Start the "new conversation" to set yourself free and find fulfillment: *"What you think of me is none of my business."*

ASK YOURSELF:

1. How am I beating myself up in the aftermath of my Lifeblow?

2. What am I saying to myself that leaves me feeling down about myself?

3. Relative to my challenge, what am I proud of myself for doing or saying?

4. Relative to my Lifeblow, who am I proud of myself for being?

5. How have I allowed myself to be negatively influenced by the thinking of others?

CHAPTER 11

WAY #5: ACCEPT YOUR LIFEBLOW
FOR BETTER AND WORSE

"Life could be worse AND always get better."

AFTER A LIFEBLOW, IT IS HUMAN NATURE TO START COMPARING ourselves to people we know and inevitably find evidence that we are faced with a situation that is more challenging than that of any other person we know. *"I've got it worse than everyone else"* becomes our reactive TRUTH; but we are sadly mistaken. One moment from now can bring a Lifeblow to someone we know, who is currently living in perfect bliss. Another possibility is that many of the "everybody elses," have become very good at the process in this book. Perhaps they have gotten very good at "happening to life" in the midst of their challenging circumstances. In the fulfilling life they are creating, maybe it doesn't appear that a Lifeblow ever happened.

Regardless of whether someone has had a Lifeblow on the same level as yours, or when they had it, or how well they are handling it, when you think your life is worse than everyone else's, you are mistaken. There are a lot of people in the world. The number of people we know is miniscule compared to the number of people we don't know. Practically speaking, there are people in the world who have overcome or are dealing with every conceivable Lifeblow and difficult situation, including one like yours, maybe even worse. Even if you are thinking that your challenge might be impossible to overcome, other people have felt the same way, and some of them have started enough "new conversations" to wake up in a brighter light with a reason to smile.

While we struggle at our personal ground zero, one thing that makes it very difficult to let go of our reactive TRUTH, "I have it worse than everyone else," is our natural tendency to withdraw, alienate ourselves, and avoid interaction with other people. On one hand, withdrawing can be part of a healthy healing process. We can withdraw for the purpose of expressing our feelings fully, or to reflect, soul search, pray, or read a book. Any of these could help significantly with healing and creating fulfillment after a Lifeblow.

Many times, however, our withdrawing is a reaction with no purpose or intention to make progress along our journey of "Getting Up When Life Blows Us Down." When that's the case, our seclusion provides the perfect environment to hold onto our OLD TRUTH that no one has it worse and build a case about why life's not fair. During the first weeks in the hospital, I was withdrawn in the above manner and feeling very sorry for myself. I lay in bed stewing inside, wallowing all day, day in and day out, in my reactive TRUTH:

> *"Nothing could be worse than being shot, confined to a hospital bed, and unable to move or get up for a few months. Everyone else is so lucky to not have to deal with this situation, these questions about the future, this pain, no cable TV, and these bed sores and bed pans."*

With regard to the other patients on my floor, I was still convinced that my situation was worse, because I was thinking, *"At least they can get out of bed."*

My continuous reinforcement of this negative TRUTH made it impossible to re-direct my energy and enjoy the company of family and friends, begin a healing process, or make room for "new conversations" that could have helped. Because I was confined to my hospital room in traction, and physically unable to move, it was easy to stay withdrawn, shut off from the world and all my sources of healing and strength. Since I couldn't see beyond the walls of my hospital room, I rarely saw other patients, with the exception of an occasional passerby in the hall outside my doorway. I was alone in my misery and had become a full-fledged victim of my Lifeblow.

Two weeks before being released from the hospital, my pity party about having it worse than everyone else ended abruptly. My final surgery had been completed, and I was put in a body cast. The biggest difference between these last few weeks in the hospital, compared to the first few months, was that I gained some mobility. After being put in the cast I could be helped out of bed to sit in a wheelchair. I distinctly remember the first time I rose to sit on the edge of my bed. I was facing the window and as I stood, my eyes rose to a level where I could see the lower floors of the buildings outside my window, as well as the street, which had been blocked from view by the windowsill when I was lying down. This new scenery was a very pleasant change, and I couldn't wait to get into the wheelchair and escape from my room!

As soon as I got out of the confines of that little hospital room, every inch of hallway brought new views of new things and new people. I soon discovered that the more I moved around, the more I saw, and the more I saw, the better I felt.

This change of scenery was exhilarating, like a breath of fresh air suddenly enhanced by the sweet smell of whale breath. My new mobility lifted my spirits and with exposure to new people, I didn't have to wheel myself around on that hospital floor for very long, before I started a "new conversation":

LIFE COULD BE WORSE AND CAN ALWAYS GET BETTER.

During the last few weeks before being released, I had an encounter with another patient that had a huge impact on me. I met a man in therapy who had been walking to work a few months earlier, and slipped on an icy sidewalk. He had fallen, broken his back, and was paralyzed from his waist down. Two days before I met him, he woke up at home and suddenly noticed that he was moving his big toe. His doctors now had him back in the hospital and they were pouring the therapy on, in an attempt to bring movement to the rest of his body. We shared our stories with one another and during our visit he said something to me with a look on his face, neither of which I will ever forget. He had the look of hope that looks the same on all human beings — regardless of their age, sex, culture, or nationality. He had the look of someone longing for and dreaming of better days.

He grabbed me by the arm, looked at me in the eye, and with tears in his eyes and a huge smile on his face, said "Bill, man, maybe I will get to walk again."

At that stage I knew I was going to walk again. I related to the following quote by an unknown author, *"I cried because I had no shoes until I saw a man who had no feet."* My perspective was that "Life could be worse." His perspective, as evidenced by his ability to move his toe, was "Life can always get better." In the same moment of the same encounter, those two uplifting perspectives were at work in the "new conversation": *"Life could be worse and can always get better."*

This "new conversation" provided an uplifting perspective about my current state of affairs and positive expectancy for the days ahead. It enabled me to take steps further and further away from my victim state and toward the more fulfilling life I wanted. I am not suggesting that I believe in feeling better at someone else's expense. I am certainly not encouraging that attitude. I'm simply saying that there are many scenarios we can identify, which put our Lifeblow in an encouraging new light. Every Lifeblow experience could be worse and involve more hurt, pain, anguish, frustration, and upset. Gaining that perspective can do a world of good for our sunken spirits.

The more I held this "new conversation", the more I noticed a myriad of other ways my situation could be worse. I could have lost my leg. I could have lost my job. I could have been paralyzed. I could have been in a coma. I could have bled to death. I could have been with a loved one who was hurt or killed. I could have died in surgery. I could have been confined to a hospital bed for six months, a year, even longer. The car that swerved to miss me could have hit me instead. The robber could have taken more money. I could be without family and friends who visited, called, and shared their love. Each of these scenarios represented an expanded version for me about how *"Life could be worse."*

This truth is enhanced by focusing on the ways our life can be, or has been, improved after our Lifeblow. My life is better since being shot because of my awareness for what can happen in any given moment and my resulting appreciation for people and things that are easily taken for granted. My life is better because of the lessons I have learned about reacting and responding, how to avoid a repeat, and the power of vision and purpose. These are but a *few* of the gifts that lifted me up from my personal ground zero and make a positive difference in my life every day.

As all of these "new conversations" began working in my life, my spirit of giving was awakened and I abundantly received more gifts necessary for healing. It came in the form of quality time with other people. They had been there all along, but I hadn't been there in a way that allowed them in — to work in my life. I reconnected with family and friends and received their love. I received smiles, kind words, and company from other patients and began making friends with nurses who had provided the same gifts all along.

Nurses started coming to my room, not to give me a pill or a shot, but because they saw my room as a refuge — a place to get away from the negativity and depression that existed on the rest of the hospital floor. They knew my room was a place where they could let their guard down, relax, and smile. We connected on a level that drove our relationship far beyond that of simply patient/caregiver. We laughed together, shared our lives with one another, and experienced the power of my changed attitude together. Where there was none in me before, a new light had been ignited, which spread like wildfire. Collectively, all of us illuminated the darkness that I brought to the hospital on the morning of September 28. Experiencing that turn-around, is <u>knowing</u> *"Life can always get better."*

Since the terrorist attacks, we've seen evidence of this *truth* in numerous examples for how our lives could be worse and also get better after a Lifeblow. On one hand, although the attacks were the worst in the history of the United States, there are some statistics that came out of New York, Washington, DC, and Pennsylvania that demonstrate how the attacks could have been worse. One news reporter stated that "approximately 50,000 people worked in the Twin Towers of the World Trade Center, yet 4000 people are listed missing." That means 92% of the people targeted, survived the attack. When we consider the numbers of people who died at the World Trade Center, compared to what might have been, we realize *"Life could be worse."*

In addition to that perspective, consider that there could have been five or six or ten planes hijacked. What if all the airports hadn't been shut down? Many hundreds or thousands of people could have been killed. Planes could have been used as missiles in Dallas, Chicago, Los Angeles, Atlanta, Las Vegas, or New Orleans. Considering those possibilities, along with the fact that each of the planes that did crash, could have been full, at least 1014 more people could be dead today. The terrorist attacks could have been a LOT worse.

On the other hand, positive unintended consequences have emerged worldwide in the wake of the attacks. With people from eighty-three different countries affected by the attacks, the smoking rubble and smoldering ruins have inspired a commitment to build a more united world and work together to improve conditions for children in impoverished countries.

Everyone clearly sees the link between terrorism and poverty. In countries where children are living in poverty, without education and opportunities, they are much more easily influenced by terrorist mindsets. When people are uneducated and no opportunities exist to better themselves, it becomes easier to carry resentment and buy into such beliefs as "wealthy countries and their people are 'the enemy'." With this new collective focus among a united world, much more will be done to address issues of starvation, disease, and neglect, and improve the lives of children around the world. Children, who might otherwise join a terrorist group to gain a sense of belonging, will make different decisions in a more supportive, positive, and healthy environment. *"Life can always get better."*

Things are also better in America. As the minister of the church I attend said after the attacks, "Our hearts were broken on Tuesday, but not broken down. They were broken open." They were broken open to caring, compassion, love, acceptance, kindness, and understanding. Generally speaking, we are more patriotic, united, supportive, caring, compassionate, loving, and kind to one another.

After the attacks, sacrifice and service, superceded selfishness, as evidenced by countless examples of selfless giving of time, talents, effort, energy, money, ideas, and blood. We were united and differences in culture, religion, nationality, sex, and age were set aside as trivial matters compared to what is really important. We were reconnected to our core values of family, life, freedom, peace, and safety. Our political interests were replaced by human interests. Perhaps it was said best by a hospice nurse from Philadelphia, who, upon arriving in New York two and a half weeks after the attacks, said she immediately felt a sense of community and commented, "It's more quiet than I ever remember. People are more patient and calm. They aren't honking their horns. It's a city at its best."

During the chaos and confusion on September 11, on one of the worst days in the history of America, I doubt that anyone was thinking about the improved world that was emerging; however, in some ways THAT world did very quickly. Depending on how big or recent your Lifeblow is, it might be unimaginable to think how life could be worse or get any better. Perhaps the best place to start is believing that "Life can always get better than the one I'm experiencing at my personal ground zero." By focusing on that possibility, even a tiny bit of movement in that direction can be uplifting. It was for a paralyzed man who noticed movement in his big toe.

Your world and mood at your personal ground zero can improve too, when you start the "new conversation": *"Life could be worse and can always get better."*

ASK YOURSELF:

1. How could my Lifeblow be worse for myself?

2. How could my Lifeblow be worse for my family?

3. How can I complete the following sentences?

   I'm glad I'm not _____.
   I'm glad I don't _____.
   I'm glad I still _____.

   Completing these three simple sentences, over and over,
   helps you see how easy it would be to take out a piece of
   notebook paper and fill it with all the reasons you are
   fortunate. After filling one side of the page, it wouldn't be
   far fetched to say you could then turn the page over, and
   keep writing more and more scenarios for how life could
   be worse. Take out a piece of notebook paper and fill it
   with the ways your Lifeblow could be worse.

4. Looking at the list you wrote, for each way you have
   identified your situation could be worse, ask, "How could
   my situation be worse than that?"

5. How has my life improved as a result of my Lifeblow?

6. How is it possible for my life to improve as a result of my
   challenge?

CHAPTER 12

WAY #6: ADOPT AN ATTITUDE OF GRATITUDE

"I am thankful for all I am and all I have."

O UR HUMAN CONDITION IS TO TAKE THINGS FOR GRANTED. WE GET comfortable in our lives and forget how fortunate we are: to be who we are and have what we have. We lose our sense of gratitude for the abundance in our life. Sometimes Lifeblows change all that — sometimes they don't. It depends on the person and it depends on the Lifeblow.

When our reactions are negative and unproductive, they are often grounded in a very strong focus on our loss and lack, which have resulted from our Lifeblow. When our attention is focused on our loss and lack, it simply isn't possible to see the abundance in our life and develop an attitude of gratitude. While I was in the hospital and feeling angry and sorry for myself, all of my energy was directed in a selfish manner. I focused on the loss and lack that had been brought about by my experience of being shot. During the majority of my hospital stay, I could have readily pointed out all the things I lost by being shot.

My reactive conversation about my losses, included:

> *"Oh, this is great. I'm stuck in this bed, confined in traction. This existence is like living in a prison cell, maybe worse. At least in prison, people get to walk around. I've lost my freedom. I've lost my ability to work. I've lost all the enjoyment I got out of my activities outside of work — working out, socializing, playing golf, traveling, and visiting friends. I've lost, I've lost, I've lost."*

Needless to say, this conversation added significantly to my misery and anger. The first mindset shifts I remember having in the area of gratitude, was when I developed the blood clot in my lung and met the nurse who had been in the emergency room on the morning of September 28. Because of the way she looked at me when telling me how lucky I was to be alive, I was never the same. She helped me re-focus on my blessings and got me back in touch with how easy it is to be appreciative for how fortunate I am to have an opportunity to live another day on this earth. Getting robbed and shot has given me a sense of gratitude for having another day to enjoy my friends and loved ones. My mother has said that at times I was very pleasant in the hospital. I believe she was also saying, "It's rather difficult to be unpleasant at the same time you are being grateful for being alive" and holding the "new conversation":

I AM THANKFUL FOR ALL I AM AND ALL I HAVE.

Marcel Proust said, "The real voyage of discovery consists not in seeking new landscapes, but in having new eyes." **Adopting an attitude of gratitude gives us new eyes that enable us to re-discover those things we have been taking for granted.**

During the process of developing my attitude of gratitude, and while learning how to forgive the robber, I noticed something different about the four walls of my hospital room. Up until then, they had simply represented prison walls that did nothing but confine and take my freedom away. I had been so absorbed in my pity party and negative focus that I had missed the true meaning of those four walls. For the first time since being admitted, I noticed what they represented. They were covered with cards and banners from people who had sent their well wishes. The two tables in the room and the windowsill were covered with plants and flowers that friends and family sent to show their love, support, and encouragement.

Once I recognized the same walls as "giving," I was able to experience them as a source of strength and renewal. With that huge shift in perspective, it was impossible NOT to have an attitude of gratitude for the abundance in my life, especially all the people in my cheering section. The people who, after a Lifeblow, come to our side, put their arms around us, pat us on the back, give us a hug and a kiss, and say, "Hang in there. You're not alone. Be tough. We're pulling for you. Be strong. We support you. Most of all, we love you." When we notice our gifts that we've been taking for granted, we've started the "new conversation": *"I am thankful for all I am and all I have."*

My attitude of GRATITUDE for loved ones and not being killed or paralyzed, led to my awareness of many other reasons to be grateful. Instead of being mad about the police not catching the robber, I became thankful for what they were doing to try to catch him. The policemen were dressing up, undercover, going out at all hours of the day and night, using ATMs to lure the robber out. While doing that, they arrested five people who tried to rob them at gunpoint. Although none of the arrested people was the guy who shot me, I realized the police were <u>risking their lives</u> to ensure our safety! I felt thankful for doctors, nurses, and advancements in medicine that enabled me to keep my leg. Instead of being upset about the car that didn't stop when I was lying in the middle of the street, I felt thankful for the person who did call the ambulance after hearing my calls for help. I felt thankful for the ambulance that arrived and the paramedics who arrived with it. I felt thanks and appreciation for my employer and the job that was waiting for me. My life was transformed with the "new conversation": *"I am thankful for all I am and all I have."*

We have so much to be grateful for regarding the terrorist attacks. As was discussed in the last chapter, the attacks could have been much worse and killed many more people. I am thankful and have a tremendous amount of gratitude for being an American and living in the United States. I'm grateful that I live in a society where terrorism is the exception and not the norm. I am thankful for the freedoms I had been taking for granted before the attacks.

I am also thankful for being a part of a nation and worldwide community of people who take care of one another in times of need. I am thankful for the outpouring of selfless giving by Americans. Thousands of people gave financial support. People gave their time and talent, such as the doctor working in a small hospital near Ground Zero who worked around the clock for four days. And what about the outpouring of effort and energy by volunteers, hospital staff, police officers, and fire and rescue workers who worked to exhaustion with the attitude that "each of us needs all of us." I am grateful to be part of a country and part of a people as committed as that to their values. *"I am thankful for all I am and all I have."*

Regardless of your current circumstances, and where your Lifeblow has left you, you are alive and enjoying some, if not all, the miraculous faculties of your body that are easy to take for granted. Saint Augustine said, "People travel to wonder at the height of the mountains, at the huge waves of the seas, at the long course of the rivers, at the vast compass of the ocean, at the circular motion of the stars, and yet they pass by themselves without wondering." Consider the following passage by Og Mandino, taken from his book, *The Greatest Miracle In The World*. If you are like me, you'll be left with a sense of wonder and gratitude for how we have been created.

> *"Are you blind? No, you can see and the hundred million receptors in your eyes enable you to enjoy the magic of a leaf, a snowflake, a pond, an eagle, a child, a cloud, a rose, a star, a rainbow . . . and the look of love. Count one blessing.*
>
> *Are you deaf? Can a baby laugh or cry without your attention? No. You can hear and the twenty-four thousand fibers built into each ear vibrate to the wind in the trees, the majesty of an opera, waves on the shore, children at play, and the words "I love you." Count another blessing.*
>
> *Are you mute? Do your lips move and only bring forth spittle? No. You can speak, as no other creature on earth. Your words can calm the angry, uplift the despondent, goad the quitter, cheer the unhappy, warm the lonely, praise the worthy, encourage the defeated, teach the ignorant . . . and say "I love you." Count another blessing.*
>
> *Is your heart stricken? Does it leak and strain to maintain your life? No. Your heart is strong. Touch your chest and feel its rhythm, pulsating, hour after hour, day and night, thirty-six million beats each year, year after year, asleep or awake, pumping your blood through more than sixty-thousand miles of veins, arteries, and tubing . . . pumping more than six-hundred thousand gallons each year. Man has never created such a machine. Count another blessing.*

Is your body diseased? Do people turn in horror when you approach? No. Your body is a marvel, needing only that you tend to it in a caring way. You can move. You can stretch and run and dance and work, for within you there are 500 muscles, 200 bones, and seven miles of nerve fiber — all synchronized to do your bidding. Within your five quarts of blood are twenty-two trillion blood cells and within each cell are millions of molecules and within each molecule is an atom oscillating at more than ten million times each second. Every second, two million of your blood cells die to be replaced by two million more in a resurrection that has continued since your first birth. As it has always been inside your body, so it is with your skin. Count another blessing.

Are you feeble of mind? Can you no longer think for yourself? No. Your brain is the most complex structure in the universe. Within its three pounds are thirteen billion nerve cells to help you file away every perception, every sound, every taste, every smell, and every action you have experienced since the day you were born. To assist your brain in the control of your body, there are dispersed — four million pain-sensitive structures, five hundred thousand touch detectors, and more than two hundred thousand temperature detectors. Count another blessing.

You are a precious specimen. Never, in all the seventy billion humans who have walked this planet since the beginning of time has there been anyone exactly like you. Never, until the end of time, will there be another such as you. You are the rarest thing in the world. Within you is enough atomic energy to destroy any of the world's great cities . . . and rebuild them. You are powerful! You are rich! We have just counted your wealth! You have so much going for you, why are you walking around looking so sad, defeated, rejected, and miserable? Why did you deceive yourself that you were powerless to change your life? Are you without talent, senses, abilities, pleasures, instincts, sensations, and pride? Are you without hope?

You have so much. Your blessings overflow your cup. What rich man, old and sick, feeble and helpless, would not exchange all the gold in his vault for the blessings you have taken for granted and treated so lightly?"

In the words of Ralph Waldo Emerson, "What lies behind us and what lies before us are tiny matters compared to what lies within us." As is the case for after-Lifeblow lessons and newfound wisdom, it's not possible to take an inventory of all we have and all we are, and then put a dollar value on them.

How much money would you take for your body? How much money would you take for your eyes and ears? Would you take a million dollars? Would you take five million? How about ten million? What about your lungs or heart or brain? How much money would you take for them? Forget about your body for a moment. What's it worth to live in this great country? What kind of price tag would you put on that? Where would you rather live? None of us ever read about a group of Americans who have been rescued in the middle of the ocean, hanging on a makeshift raft while trying to get to a better country. What's your freedom worth? What are your loved ones worth? How much would you take to give them up?

It doesn't take long to see how absurd this line of questioning is. We are priceless beings with priceless lives.

One day, while wheeling myself up and down the hallway, I entered the room of a woman. Both of her arms and legs were in traction. Her eyes were open and as I got closer to her bed, she looked at me but was hardly able to make a sound. I smiled, but her expression never changed. For a moment, I thought she was dead. I slowly turned around and quietly left. When I got into the hallway, one of my favorite nurses was nearby and I asked about the lady. I learned that she was heavily medicated because nearly every bone in her body was broken. She had thrown herself off the overpass of an interstate, into oncoming traffic, to try to commit suicide. When those words hit my ears, I thought about her mental and physical state, and heard myself say, *"I am thankful for all I am and all I have."*

That left me thinking about the day before when I met the paralyzed man and first began thinking about how fortunate I was. I thought back on the moment I reached the emergency room. I saw myself lying there before losing consciousness, watching a monitor that nurses were using to determine the degree of artery damage and ultimately the fate of my leg. As I rolled down the hall and into my room, I realized I could easily be returning from therapy to learn how to walk on a prosthetic leg. Even if that were the case, I would still have the use of my other leg. This perspective made me realize how my injury paled in comparison to being paralyzed and how ungrateful I had been.

My encounters not only had me realize it could always be worse. It also gave me an attitude of gratitude and an enormous sense of fulfillment. **Take advantage of the opportunity to be fulfilled by being thankful.** You'll shut down the blaring volume of your pity party and find peace and quiet when you start the "new conversation": *"I am thankful for all I am and all I have."*

ASK YOURSELF:

1. Who have I been taking for granted?

2. What have I been taking for granted?

3. Considering my mind and body, what am I thankful for?

4. If asked to identify five people I am grateful for TODAY, who would they be?

5. If asked to identify five things I am grateful for TODAY, what would they be? (Consider your health, family, friends, career, support group, faith, etc.)

CHAPTER 13

WAY #7: EXPRESS YOUR FEELINGS care-FULLY

"To feel is to heal."

EVERY DAY OF OUR LIFE, ALL OF OUR THOUGHTS, FEELINGS, AND actions, constitute energy spent to create a result at the end of the day. As people wanting to have a fulfilling life experience and cause more desired outcomes, it is critical to be aware of how we are spending our energy. This book is designed to help you become aware of two things, how your reactive nature and energy sometimes creates unfulfilling results and how you can create new results by redirecting your energy.

So far, we've covered how the important first step in that redirection process is stopping our harmful reactive energy. We follow that with shifting our perspective and starting "new conversations", which provide a source of new *thought energy*, which in turn generates new *feeling energy* that positively impacts how we spend our time. In that sense, our self-control serves us well because it produces *life-giving* energy, or energy that gives us more of what we want in life; however, we must be very careful not to overlook what also happens when we stop our reaction. When we stop our reaction, we stop the expression of our feelings. In the short run, that's okay; however, over time our non-expression of feelings is very limiting.

Marcel Proust said, "We are healed of a suffering only by experiencing it in full," meaning that *healing* requires experiencing our feelings and expressing them carefully for the purpose of healing.

That's why the title of this chapter is, "Express Your Feelings care-FULLY." In the process of "Getting Up When Life Blows You Down," it's critical to expand our definition of self-control. Exercising self-control goes way beyond preventing negative reactions. It also includes "*FULLY* experiencing the feelings that drive our reaction by taking *care* in how, when, where, and with whom we express them." Sometimes we make the mistake of having incredible self control to stop our reaction, without ever experiencing our feelings FULLY. Both are keys to rising out of our personal ground zero.

When we stop an unhealthy reaction, we have shut down our expression of feelings. As soon as we stop our reaction, we separate ourselves from the natural feelings our Lifeblow generated. Our "new conversations" generate new feelings, but we must avoid repressing the natural feelings we have about our challenge. Those feelings remain and "Getting Up When Life Blows Us Down" requires that we NOT ignore, suppress, or discount them. We must FULLY experience them in an appropriate manner. Before we cover *why* fully experiencing our feelings is so important, let's take a look at some common reasons for holding our emotions back.

We don't experience our feelings for many reasons. Challenging *change* experiences produce a sense of LOSS in human beings. Suddenly, our life is not the same. The sense of loss varies, depending on the nature of the event and how much our lives have been altered. As a result of our loss, we experience feelings of hurt and sadness along with anger and fear. Sometimes our human tendency is to avoid experiencing feelings of hurt. Society conditions us, especially as men, that crying shows we are weak. Women can also be influenced by this conditioning. Instead of compromising the perception people have of our toughness and strength, and risking embarrassment, we "stuff" our feelings and vow "not to go there."

Another reason we avoid our experience of feelings of hurt, is because we associate letting go and feeling as something that will generate more pain. When we are already in pain, our logic tells us to avoid more. After Lifeblows, one assumption we make about avoiding further pain is that isolating ourselves from other people will help. If we keep ourselves isolated, we can avoid conversations and talking about what is going on inside. Talking about feelings IS an expression of how we feel and opens the door for deeper feelings to rise up and come out. Instead of risking that, we avoid pain by avoiding interaction with other people.

In some cases, we tell ourselves that a challenge is too small to generate whatever feelings we have. We might start labeling our feelings as positive or negative, good or bad, and right or wrong, thinking that we should avoid, suppress, and hold back the feelings we have identified as "negative," "bad," and "wrong." We consciously decide to "be strong" and "move on." We see the "moving on" without *feeling*, as personal growth; that the better we get at doing that, the better off we'll be, as if there is something wrong with the way we feel.

Nothing could be further from the truth. There is never, ever, ever a *wrong* way to feel. Suggesting that there is something wrong with your feelings, no matter what they are, would be like suggesting there is something wrong with sleeping. Each is an integral part of being human and each is necessary for achieving peak performance in life.

Granted, there are a few important considerations. There are variables in each, which do effect the quality of our life. For instance, how, when, and where you sleep certainly can make a difference in the results you create. If you fell asleep with your head bent in an awkward way, you might wake up with a pain in the neck that causes you trouble the next day. Falling asleep at work or in class might also get you in trouble. Falling asleep while driving a car might get you in some serious trouble.

Feelings are like that. Feelings don't create undesired outcomes. Feelings we avoid and thus unconsciously keep without changing, play a big role in what we create after a Lifeblow. Creating fulfillment requires balance between stopping an unhealthy reaction, facing our feelings, and taking care in how, when, where, and with whom we express them. A full acceptance and acknowledgment of responsibility for our feelings is also critical for preventing a disaster.

I once heard a psychologist use the metaphor that our feelings are like the air in a beach ball and holding our feelings inside is a lot like holding a beach ball under water. It takes a lot of energy to suppress our feelings. Like air, the natural path of feelings is to rise to the surface. When we hold our feelings in, we are interrupting the design of how we have been created to realize our highest potential. **Feelings surface because HEALING requires letting them go.** The "letting go" *is* healing. Experiencing feelings, including those that generate tears, doesn't cause more pain. The source of our pain is not in the talking about feelings and releasing them. Our source of pain is in what the Lifeblow means to us and what we choose to believe about it and do about it. When we cry, we release the pain inside and allow it to flow out. That's the wisdom behind the "new conversation":

TO FEEL IS TO HEAL.

When your energy goes into suppressing and holding back, you spend a lot of thought energy holding back feeling energy that is meant to be released. Depending on how much energy you spend this way, you can wear yourself into a state of exhaustion. When you continuously feel tired and worn out, even when you are getting plenty of sleep, your attempt to disguise and repress your feelings might be a major contributor. Holding your feelings in over time is *life-taking* energy, because you have less energy and ability to create desired outcomes.

During my weeks in the hospital after being shot, my pent-up feelings prevented me from healing. I kept my tears inside in the spirit of being tough and staying strong. Each time I visualized beating the robber, I played the tough guy, but was internalizing my anger and sadness and keeping it inside. Much of my energy was being spent generating more anger and then suppressing it, generating more, and suppressing it. I had a beach ball full of anger inside that wanted to surface. By internalizing it, not only did my focus prevent me from creating "new conversations" and gain a new perspective, I had nothing else to give away.

As human beings, we are like a pitcher that can be filled with spring water . . . or acid. The pitcher will hold either, but if it is full of acid, we can't pour a cool glass of water. We are like a pitcher. As a human being, we can hold all feelings, including love and joy; however, if we are full of anger, hatred, and resentment, we aren't able to pour out much of anything else. Bitterness and anger are our contribution to the world when we are bitter and angry. We can't give away what we don't possess inside. When I was in the hospital full of hate and anger, there was little room for love, gratitude, appreciation, or joy. I've described how I sabotaged relationships by not speaking to my parents or welcoming friends who came to visit. They didn't deserve that, but I had nothing else to give away.

When we are full of stored-up feelings that our self-control hasn't allowed to flow out, we not only limit what we can give away, we also set ourselves up to have an outpouring of feelings and reactive energy, otherwise known as an overreaction to something that happens. When we hold our feelings in, over time, we get so full of repressed feelings that our beach ball is filled to capacity. Our feelings are just under the surface. The next smallest upsetting event and Lifeblow becomes a force that pops our beach ball. We've reached a breaking point and our feelings leak out, sometimes slowly and sometimes in a rush, like water through a dam that no longer has the strength to confine it. Our self-control begins to crumble under the pressure of all we've been holding back, and we are no longer able to be careful in the expression of our feelings, thus expressing them in very destructive ways.

You may remember in early November 2001 — when New York City mandated that the search at Ground Zero would no longer go on around the clock because of budgetary constraints. That command went against the very core of who firemen are and what firemen wake up to do, so some resisted and nine firemen were arrested. In addition to the firemen's resistance being a result of their commitment and sense of purpose being threatened, it is likely that their anger from the attacks was also coming out. They were full of feelings, but had been working around the clock. They hadn't stopped to really begin any grieving process since the attacks.

At some point all their feelings would have to come out and be experienced in order to heal. When told they couldn't work around the clock and heard that they were being stopped from fulfilling their purpose, they became angry. The unexpected change in procedure was a mini-Lifeblow. There wasn't any more room in their beach balls for the feelings that came up. As a result, some of them exploded. In the end, nine firemen were arrested for how they expressed their anger in resisting the order. The good news is that the same nine firemen were not charged because they were doing what they took an oath to do, fulfilling their unselfish purpose.

When our beach ball of suppressed feelings is beyond capacity

and starts coming out, we have no resistance left to stop our potentially disastrous reaction. That happened to me a few times in the
hospital. One Saturday afternoon when I was still confined to the bed
in traction, I turned on the TV to watch a college football game
between two top-ranked teams in the country. For weeks, I had been
thinking about this game. Watching it would be a wonderful break in
the monotony of a typical day in the hospital. At the magic hour, I
turned on the television, found the channel, and saw some high
school bands marching down a street. I thought this must be a pre-
game show. Then it dawned on me. The bands I was watching were
local. I changed channels to make sure I hadn't made a mistake, and
figured out moments later that the game had been preempted to
cover a holiday parade that I could almost watch out of my hospital
room window. I got furious! My beach ball of stored anger had no
room to hold any more and, like the firemen, I exploded.

I grabbed an overhead bar that ran the length of my bed and
helped keep my leg in place and tried to bend it. Then I smashed the
TV remote on the floor. Stored up anger was rushing out of me, like
steam from a whistling kettle of boiling water. I was in the middle of
a serious overreaction, completely unaware and out of control. One of
the nurses heard my tantrum from a few rooms away, and came
flying around the corner. Just as I was reaching for my lunch cart to
get my hands on something else to throw, she pulled it away just in
time, saying, "Hold on, Bill. Hold On!"

She quickly pushed the cart into the hallway and returned in a
few seconds with an unused plastic plate. Slowly walking toward me
with the plate, she pointed at me and in a very stern voice, said, "Wait
until I am out of the way and give you the signal." She handed the
plate to me and then hurried out and ducked behind the wall separating my room from the hallway. Peering into my room and
gesturing toward the open door, she calmly said, "Bill, the coast is
clear. I want you to throw that plate out here as hard as you can."
After hesitating for a moment, I took that plate and sailed it out my
doorway like a Frisbee, smashing it against the wall outside. Surprised
that it didn't break, she picked up the plate, brought it back, and held
it out, saying, "You want more?" I nodded yes, so she handed it to me
again, and said, "Go ahead. Get it out of your system." I let it fly again

and again. . . . Each time I sailed that plate against the wall, I felt a little better. My release was an outlet that prevented me from continuing to recycle my anger over and over. *"To feel is to heal."*

Later on, I was able to look back at that afternoon of indoor Frisbee throwing, and learn a couple of great lessons about the expression of feelings. One of those lessons, I'll discuss immediately. The other, I'll disclose in chapter 14. The first lesson I learned is that the game, not being televised, didn't generate all the anger that rose up and out of me that afternoon. My anger over that one issue simply triggered an enormous amount of anger that had built up over time as I repressed it. I had no room inside to store any more anger. My beach ball was full, so I erupted like a volcano. I was so full of anger that I had nothing else to give away on the one holiday set aside specifically for giving thanks — Thanksgiving Day.

Although we are greatly served by having self-control in the short-term, so we don't do something we later regret, if we are going to be our best over the long haul, we must also take time to honestly acknowledge our feelings and experience and express them with care. That is self control — where our feelings are neither repressed nor carelessly expressed. Without making that move, feelings build up and come out later at inopportune times and in inappropriate ways. **We create short-term desired outcomes with our control, and create long-term fulfillment by letting our controlled feelings go, very *care-FULLY*.** Expressing your feelings care-FULLY means taking care in the full expression of your feelings. We can be MAD and go hit a punching bag OR go hit another human being. It's the same feeling, we're just channeling it differently. "Getting Up When Life Blows You Down" means allowing feelings to rise up without excusing your behavior when they do.

A Chinese proverb says, "If you are patient in one moment of anger, you will escape a hundred days of sorrow." Anger is like fear, in that it is NOT a bad emotion, but it's not a pleasant one either. Anger is energy that requires patience, followed by an appropriate focus of expression and intention on healing. Fortunately, the nurse arrived in time to help me accomplish that. She helped me express my anger in a safe and monitored way. It's a good thing that I couldn't bend the bar that supported my leg. That likely would have led to unbearable pain. Because of the nurse's arrival, I didn't hurt myself, or someone else, in an unchecked reactive state of throwing things and regret the outcome I created. When we are so full of anger that we are seeing red, we can't and don't see the consequences of being that mad.

When we speak while angry, we might just give the best speech we ever regret. Just because we have no choice about our Lifeblow generated feelings, doesn't mean we don't have a choice about how, when, where, and with whom we express those feelings for healing. That's another important dimension of self-control, and we must also accept responsibility for that part of the process. If we are going to avoid a buildup and uncontrollable outflow of expression that doesn't serve us, we must have a safe place to vent. A safe place is where we can be fully expressed without hurting ourselves and other people.

I mentioned earlier, our natural tendency to alienate ourselves after a Lifeblow. I related the subsequent alienation as limiting from the standpoint that our seclusion provides the perfect environment for not being exposed to other people, therefore enabling us to avoid the expression of feelings and hold onto our old truth that "no one has it worse than me" and "life's not fair." When secluded, we have no evidence for how our situation could be worse. One important point I want to make is that "BEING ALONE" is not a damaging element to "Getting Up When Life Blows Us Down." The damaging element to that process, lies in some of the things we do or don't do while being alone, such as those things mentioned above. The safest place to vent our feelings happens to be when we are alone. We can fully let go without being worried about what other people think, or feeling embarrassed. When we withdraw for that purpose, we create an opportunity to heal. *"To feel is to heal."*

Choosing a safe place to vent also means choosing to express our feelings with people who won't judge or blame us for letting go. Think of a time when you had a Lifeblow, but didn't cry until you saw or heard the voice of a loved one. If you've had that experience, you can recognize our natural tendency to hold some feelings in, as well as the benefit of having a truly safe place to vent your feelings. Like the nurse who provided a safe space for me to vent, it's important to have people in our life who support us in the same way, whether they lend an ear without taking it personally, help you throw a plate, or hold you as you cry. One of the blessings of true friendship is that it provides such a space when either of you need it.

During the week after the terrorist attacks, TV stations provided an outlet for people who had loved ones on the planes or who were missing after the collapse of the World Trade Center to call in and share their experience. For those of us watching TV, we saw people feeling their pain and expressing their anger, sorrow and grief. That began an important process for all of us. Not only were people directly affected by the attacks, expressing their emotions, but all of us began talking about our feelings and started allowing them to surface. While being exposed to TV and talking to people about the attacks, feelings of sadness from being shot thirteen years earlier, were awakened in me.

In interviews with firefighters who survived the collapse of the World Trade Center, many said they thought they were going to die. A few of them mentioned that when they were sure of their fate, a peaceful feeling came over them, and they held images of their family members in their minds as the way they would leave this earth. I heard a few firefighters who had been trapped in the rubble, say that while they were buried, they would see light that they thought was sunlight from the outside, but it would turn out to be another fire breaking out. Their hope would be lost. In one case a firefighter described the beams creaking above him and debris falling on his back as he was trapped and lying face down. He said he was sure he would die, but then the debris would stop falling on him. He would regain hope, only to lose it moments later when debris started falling again.

Listening to those interviews was very moving to me. I related to that very strange scenario of going back and forth in my mind, one minute thinking I would die, and the next thinking maybe everything would be okay. Remembering those moments I spent lying in the street after being shot left me in tears more than a decade later.

I attended a five-day leadership seminar in October of 2001 and was guided through a self-awareness process designed to improve my effectiveness as a leader. During the process, I got in touch with how much sorrow I had stored up since being shot. The seminar leader had created a safe space for expressing feelings —and let go I did. The tears came very easily. There was more healing for me to do. *"To feel is to heal."*

Later in the program while we were sharing our experiences, I was able to see in myself how limiting unexpressed feelings can be.

The sadness in me that had been awakened after the terrorist attacks, had been evident to everyone with whom I interacted. My feelings of sadness were as noticeable as the feelings of anger we have all seen in people clearly on the verge of exploding. By relating my unexpressed feelings to the topic of leadership, I got clear on how ineffective I was, being a sad motivational speaker. My ineffectiveness would have been every bit as great, had my beach ball been full of unexpressed feelings of anger, frustration, or discouragement. I was every bit as limited as a leader, as if I had showed up for people as a mad motivational speaker or a discouraged motivational speaker.

You are leading people in your life. Whether you're leading a seminar, a child, your family, a committee, a friend, or 10,000 employees, IF, when, where, how, and with whom you express your feelings, all play a huge part in your effectiveness as a leader. Needless to say, after gaining that awareness, I felt like a new person at the end of the leadership workshop. For that matter, I *was* a new person — all the result of safely furthering my expression of feelings, which started with watching images and interviews on television after the attacks. Whether the TV stations knew it or not, they helped me and a lot of other people a great deal. Thirteen years after the shooting, I expressed pent-up feelings that had been limiting me in life. I was reminded of the importance of taking time to express our feelings care-FULLY. The quicker we let our Lifeblow generated feelings go, the quicker we can be our best in this life. *"To feel is to heal."*

I described earlier how I contributed to relationship breakdowns with the lack of positive and healthy communication. While isolating myself, I took myself away from the healing power of being with other people and talking about my experience and feelings. I took myself away from releasing the feeling energy necessary to heal. After adopting the attitude of gratitude for the people in my cheering section, I opened up. That helped me redirect my feeling energy from suppressing to expressing, and opened the door to release some of my pain.

The leadership seminar reminded me of another important part of the healing process. After releasing some of the feeling energy I had been keeping inside, I was physically exhausted, but in a very healthy way. If you've ever had the experience of the outpouring of feelings, where the tears keep coming and coming, you know what I mean.

You have been physically and emotionally drained. "I cried myself to sleep" is a phrase that says it all about what happens when we release pain that we've been storing up. Draining ourselves spends a ton of energy that needs to be restored. That's the reason it is so very important, after a release, to take time to do things in order to re-energize.

How do we re-energize? In addition to sleeping, we can engage in a favorite activity that brings us joy and fills the space we have drained. We can go away to the beach or mountains, visit a museum, watch an uplifting movie, go dancing, or ride a bike or a horse. We can go fishing, ride a roller coaster, visit a spa, play a favorite game or sport, visit friends, take a bubble bath, walk through the woods, or watch the sun rise or set. We can play with a puppy or take a drive through the country listening to our favorite music. These are but a few examples of options for re-energizing. Notice many take very little brainpower — that's the idea. My point is to do whatever it is that personally enriches your life. These pleasurable experiences revitalize you physically, mentally, and emotionally. While you are drained by the release of unexpressed feelings, you have also been *cleansed* in the process. By expressing your feelings *FULLY,* you've made room to be filled back up with life giving energy. *"To feel is to heal."*

After expressing some of my pent-up feelings of anger and sadness, I was drained and cleansed in a way that I now had room inside to receive love, support, and comfort, which are vital to additional healing and recovery. I had room inside to hold and be filled with *life-giving* energy of love and joy. Being filled with this new energy, made it possible to start more "new conversations" that generated even more *life-giving* energy, such as gratitude and appreciation. Being filled with those things not only left me feeling better — it also made it possible for me to give those things away. My life and relationships in the hospital were transformed from miserable to fulfilling by care-FULLY expressing my feelings. *"To feel is to heal."*

Several years ago, while visiting Hawaii with my family, we decided to get up at 4 AM one day to climb on a bus and ride to the top of Mount Haleakala, a dormant volcano on the island of Maui. The purpose of this trip was to have breakfast on top of the mountain while watching the sunrise, and then bike down through the rain forest and sugar cane fields, enjoying the countryside and seeing the island in a very unique way. After reaching the top of Mount

Haleakala, I felt miserable. I was uncomfortable, tired, and cold, as I stood with a group of other people in total darkness and misty rain. Had there been an option to return to the hotel and climb back into bed, I would have jumped at the opportunity.

While complaining about the cold and discomfort, suddenly the sun broke over the horizon and light was cast over a magnificent view that confirmed why our guide had described the morning as a spiritual experience. No human could ever design or create what we were looking at, and almost instantly, I no longer felt cold and tired. I realized the energy it took to get here, was well worth the trip. I was thankful I had seen the process through. By the time I climbed on my bike, the rain had stopped, the clouds were gone, and my energy was restored. As I coasted down that mountain through beautiful countryside, fulfillment was my reward.

My experience on the top of Mount Haleakala, is a great metaphor for what it is like to care-Fully express your feelings after a Lifeblow. Beginning the process of releasing feelings of sadness and hurt, is about as fun as standing in darkness on top of a mountain, cold and tired. It's extremely uncomfortable, but by going there and staying in the process long enough, the darkness ends and the clouds disappear because you have been cleansed. Light of a new day arrives, bringing with it new life energy to restore and lift your spirits. That makes your rough and draining trip very, very worthwhile. Have a good cry without asking *should I* or *why*. Live the "new conversation": *"To feel is to heal."*

ASK YOURSELF:

1. Have I/am I expressing the feelings my Lifeblow has generated? If not, or if there are more to express, where can I go to do that safely?

2. When will I express those feelings safely?

3. Where and with whom will I express those feelings safely?

4. Where have my unexpressed feelings come out in a way that didn't serve me?

5. How, when, and where can I express my feelings differently to produce more desirable outcomes?

CHAPTER 14

WAY #8: ACT BECAUSE YOU *HAVE* A FEELING, NOT BECAUSE YOU *ARE* THAT FEELING

"I choose ways I like to feel and find reasons in my life to feel THAT way."

*I*MENTIONED A SECOND LESSON LEARNED DURING MY TEMPER TANTRUM after the ballgame didn't get aired. Each time the nurse handed me the plate to throw, I became more aware that I was choosing how to express my anger. The nurse had introduced an option to me, reminding me of my power to choose how, when, where, and with whom I express my feelings. **There is a world of difference between *being* mad AND *choosing* mad, as the way we are expressing ourselves.** When I threw the TV remote to the floor, I was "being mad." When the nurse interrupted my tantrum, I saw an opportunity to choose a healthier expression and not be reckless with my feelings. When I sailed the plate through the doorway, with an assuredness that no one, including myself, would be hurt, I was "choosing to express my feelings of anger" in order to heal.

Being mad is a reactive state that can create regrettable outcomes because you are unconsciously being run by your feelings of anger. Choosing not to be mad is a responsive state, where you consciously honor your need to heal and purposefully do so by care-FULLY expressing your feelings of anger. The difference is between being a victim of your Lifeblow and getting a result you may regret AND being the victor over your Lifeblow and creating a result that you desire.

In choosing the way I expressed my anger for healing, by the time my mom got back to my room for her afternoon visit, I had safely vented my feelings. I was able to share what had happened earlier and have a sense of humor about my tantrum. I also was able to see how silly I must have looked, getting so upset about such a small thing. I was thankful the nurse had interfered with my reactive state and helped me express my anger care-FULLY. I, therefore, avoided embarrassment and regret that comes from destructive behavior, and saved the quality of my visit with my family and our afternoon together.

When I became clear on my ability to choose the expression of my feelings, I had a powerful insight into my relationship with my feelings. That insight is, I am NOT my feelings. I HAVE them. When a Lifeblow leaves us having the conversation with ourselves, "I am mad!," we are in a relationship with our "feeling of mad," as if it is an inseparable part of our identity. That relationship with our feelings leaves no chance of being anything other than mad OR doing anything other than what a mad person does. Amazing and wonderful possibilities for fulfillment open up when we really GET that we are not our feelings. We simply have them.

Relative to a Lifeblow you've had, have you ever said to yourself, "Gosh ^%#@!%^&, that makes me so mad!"? Are you saying that about your Lifeblow? At some point, all of us have that kind of thought. Lets go back to the statement, "Gosh &^%$#@, that makes me so mad!" If we take that self-talk and dissect it, we find an interesting contradiction within ourselves with regard to what we *want* vs. what we are *creating*. We want control, but let's look at what is happening with our reactionary self-talk about our Lifeblow.

The word _that_ refers to our Lifeblow or challenging experience, incident, and the people involved. Now let's look at the words "*makes me* so mad!" You are saying to yourself, the challenge "*makes me*" so mad. You are saying the challenge "*MAKES me*," "*MAKES ME*," "*MAKES ME SO MAD!*" Does that sound controlling to you? Of course it does! Because it IS controlling! When we say "Gosh *&^%$#@, that makes me so mad!" our Lifeblow is controlling us. If your challenge *makes you* mad, *makes you* hurt, or *makes you* disappointed, it's as if your Lifeblow has you by the ear, leading you to think and do what a mad, hurt, disappointed you does. It's as if your Lifeblow is making you think and feel a certain way and behave in a certain manner. That is the source of a lot of additional upset, because the less control you have, the unhappier you are.

Getting shot at the ATM *made me mad*. It happened to me and controlled my quality of life for two months. It was as if the robber had me by my earlobe, leading me around in my world, MAKING me mad, MAKING me blow off my parents, and MAKING me sabotage my productivity, performance, health, fulfillment, and peace of mind in the process. Weeks after I had been the robber's victim the first time, I was being his victim over and over again by allowing him to dictate my sabotaging behavior and regrettable results. No wonder I felt so terrible, miserable, and stressed. With my reaction, I had given away my power to be in control of myself. **A great way to "Get Up When Life Blows You Down" is to clearly see that you are NOT your feelings. You simply HAVE them.**

If a doctor performed surgery on you, and took everything she found out of your body, nowhere in the marvel of your physical body would that surgeon find, "MAD." There's not a single entity in your body-no organ, bone, or soft tissue — called "mad," "happy," "upset," "angry," "joyful," "disappointed," or "frustrated." Like beliefs, feelings don't exist in your body. Beliefs exist in your language or conversation with yourself and feelings exist in your experience of life while you are engaged in those conversations. Taking an unhealthy internal conversation away is not like taking your stomach out. You don't lose a thing. When the conversation is negative and produces unwelcome feelings, you actually gain the new possibilities that come with new and uplifting conversations. You gain the ability to feel better.

In any moment of any day, all of us are free to ask ourselves, as a human being, what feelings would I like to experience? What feelings would I like to have? From there, we can simply choose. The "new conversation" that describes this process, is:

I CHOOSE WAYS I LIKE TO FEEL AND FIND REASONS IN MY LIFE TO FEEL THAT WAY.

With this technique, we are creating our fulfillment from a different angle. Our idea of choosing usually equates to changing our

mind, but not changing our feelings. The idea of changing our feelings occurs to us as unnatural. We tend to think, "I AM my feelings. I
feel what I feel. If a shift in perspective naturally leads to a new way
of feeling, so be it." That's fine, but transformation also works the
other way. It can start by choosing feelings and developing a "new
conversation" out of that. Changing your inner environment isn't
limited to a focused redirection of your thoughts.

Transforming your life by choosing your feelings is simple.
Imagine you have in front of you, a light-grey 3 x 5 card and a dark-
grey 3 x 5 card. Now, simply *choose* one — choose the light-grey card
or the dark-grey card. Assuming you are finished choosing, you have
just demonstrated how simple it is to change your feelings. You did it!
Pat yourself on the back! Go ahead, you deserve it. Doesn't it feel
wonderful to be able to change your life by choosing your feelings!?

Why the confused look? Why the confused thoughts? You've just
demonstrated that you have the key to changing the way you feel in
an instant and "Get Up When Life Blows You Down." The mechanism
in your brain that enables you to choose a light-grey card over a dark-
grey card, or visa versa, is the same mechanism that enables you to
choose the way you think AND feel. It's the same mechanism that
enables you to focus on the up side instead of the downside; the
bright side instead of the gloomy side; or the glass half-full instead of
half-empty. It's the same mechanism that enables you to choose new
positive conversations to replace old negative conversations. It's also
the same mechanism that enables you to choose the way you feel. For
example — "happy" instead of "sad," or "excited" instead of "hopeless" or "angry."

Choosing feelings is simple; however, it isn't easy. It isn't <u>easy</u>
because of your attachment to the reasons you feel the way you do.
With every feeling you experience, you have a reason or justification
for it. The choosing part is simple, but getting unattached to your
reasons for feeling, that's another story. It's not easy because you are
so RIGHT about your reactive *truths*.

If you had asked me while in the hospital on day one, "Bill, how
do you feel?" I would have answered, "I'm mad!" If you had then
asked me, "Why do you feel mad?" I would have first looked at you
like you are an idiot, and then said with <u>much</u> conviction, "*Just*

because!" (I am my feelings). If you had asked, *"Well, because WHY?,* my answer would have been, *"Because I'm in pain." "Because I've been victimized and can't do anything to the SOB who did this." "Because I'm confined to this bed." "Because the people in the car didn't stop to help me,"* and *on and on. . . .* I would have happily continued building my case with all the reactive self-talk I've shared throughout this book. All my reasons for being mad, represent how I was attached to my feelings of mad.

As long as I was attached to being mad, I was unable to "be" any other way. Transforming your life by choosing your feelings, is only possible when you let go of your <u>attachment</u> to the reasons you are mad. You must let go of what you think is your identity. Remember, your truths and feelings about life, are not an inseparable part of who you are. Your truths and feelings don't exist like your collarbone exists. Your truths exist in your internal conversation, and your feelings exist in your experience of living while having that conversation. Another way to say it is to say that your feelings are tied to your self-talk or internal conversation or TRUTH, whichever you'd like to call them. When you recognize your relationship between your feelings and internal dialog about your Lifeblow, you can break your attachment to the feelings you are experiencing.

Remember how I would have answered your question, "Bill, why do you feel mad?" I would have told you, "I am mad BECAUSE I'm in pain. BECAUSE I've been victimized and can't do anything to the SOB who did this. BECAUSE I'm confined to this bed," and so on. Notice how I'm <u>attached</u> to my feelings of being mad, with all the reasons WHY I feel mad and am justified to feel mad. My reasons for being mad, give me my experience of being mad.

My reasons for feeling mad can be identified in the part of my reactive conversation that begins with the word BECAUSE. "I am mad BECAUSE . . ." Every word that follows the word BECAUSE in my reactive conversation, is what I'm <u>attached</u> to, or what gives me my experience of being mad. In exercising my gift of choice, I can choose to discard the part of my reactive conversation that keeps me attached to being mad. In other words, I can discard, "BECAUSE I'm in pain" and "BECAUSE I'm confined to this bed," and all my other reasons. In doing that, I'm left with a chosen conversation, "I am mad." Now I can take my power to choose, a step further. Just as I can choose one 3 x 5 card over the other, I can choose any feeling under the sun — "mad," "happy," "dumbfounded," "amazed," or "sad," etc.

Obviously, since we are after fulfillment in spite of our Lifeblow, we are interested in choosing feelings we like to experience. We don't have to choose mad. We already know what kind of life experience that choice brings. Our objective is to move away from being mad by (1) Expressing our anger with care, and (2) Filling ourselves with new feeling energy. One way we can do that is to simply choose "I am happy" or "I am fortunate." Now we can anchor ourselves to those feelings by choosing fulfilling reasons to have our chosen feeling. If we can get ourselves MORE attached to reasons for being happy, than we've been to our reasons for being mad, we are a model of a person who is creating fulfillment in spite of their Lifeblow.

I "Got Up When Life Blew Me Down" by starting the "new conversation" I CHOOSE WAYS I LIKE TO FEEL (happy, fulfilled, excited, peaceful, encouraged, fortunate, thankful, blessed, alive, loved, compassionate, appreciated, or joyful) AND FIND REASONS IN MY LIFE TO FEEL <u>THAT</u> WAY.

Having that conversation with myself, prompted me to complete the following sentence:

I feel/am _____ because _____.

          (chosen feeling)   (reason to feel that way)

And here's what I came up with:

"I am happy because I'm alive."

"I feel fortunate because no one was with me when I got robbed. I feel fortunate that a family member or friend didn't come with me and get shot or killed."

"I am blessed because I have so many people in my life who care about me and are thinking about and praying for me."

"I am excited because I am able to see and spend quality time with my family — more than I would ever see them if I wasn't confined to a bed in the hospital."

"I feel encouraged because my family and friends are being more careful using ATMs. I am encouraged because my experience has made people more aware of what can happen, which might prevent them from being victimized."

Each and every one of the above perspectives is, in fact, a "new conversation" born from choosing feelings. We can be afraid, happy, excited, challenged, surprised, angry, fortunate, encouraged, disappointed, frustrated, upset, discouraged, hopeless, hopeful, resentful, or joyful. All the above, are ways of feeling that are interchangeable. Each is just as available as all the others because each is a feeling you experience as a human who can choose.

We think there is only ONE way to be after a Lifeblow, and we miss out on many feeling options that lift us up from our personal ground zero. Notice how none of the above perspectives are farfetched. I didn't have to spend hours and hours trying to figure out what I could feel happy, encouraged, fortunate, or excited about. I didn't spend hours trying to figure out that I could actually feel happy about being alive. That perspective was just as available as "I'm mad because I'm confined to this bed," or any other TRUTH I held. I'm happy to be alive, simply wasn't the first meaning I brought to life after my Lifeblow and while in my reactive mode. Like choosing one 3 x 5 card over another, the process was simple and I created more uplifting perspectives that left me feeling a heck of a lot better and producing completely different outcomes.

Imagine sitting with me at different times while I had each of those conversations going on. You would have observed two different people. One little shift in my conversation about being shot altered my entire way of being in the hospital, as well as how other people interacted with me, and what I created the quality of my life to be. Transformation and fulfillment, comes with different choices – one being to start the "new conversation": *"I choose ways I like to feel and find reasons in my life to feel that way."*

I once spoke at a conference for NCVAN (North Carolina Victim's Assistance Network). The purpose of the conference was to enable victims to speak out about, review, and be informed of government legislation that affected and impacted victims and their families. I was asked to speak because of my shared experience as a victim of crime. After my speech, a woman introduced herself to me and we had a conversation I will never forget.

Her son had been walking home from school one day, when a car pulled up with someone riding inside who he recognized as someone he used to go to school with. They asked him if he wanted a ride, and he took them up on the offer. As it turned out, the driver of the car was a convicted murderer — out on parole. He took her son into some nearby woods and then shot him in the head, execution-style, for a $10 bill. As she shared her story, I could tell that after many years, she had never stopped feeling the loss of her son. Remarkably, as I looked into her eyes, those windows to her soul, I saw, coexisting with her pain, a light, a sparkle, a smile, a look of aliveness that transcended her pain.

The smile on her face was warm and welcoming. When she finished sharing what had happened to her son, I told her, "I am very, very sorry," and extended my arms to give her a hug. After we embraced, I swallowed hard and then fell silent because, although I shared her experience as someone impacted by crime, I could not relate to how it felt to lose a loved one, much less in such a tragic manner. I thought to myself, "What would it be like to experience that kind of loss and how has she made it through so far?"

Almost as if reading my mind, she said, "Bill, do you know how I make it through every day?"

I answered, "No, I have no idea. I can't imagine how difficult it must be."

As she began to share how she made it through each day, her answer explained the light in her eyes that I had already noticed. Her answer also reminded me of our ability to choose our feelings. She told me: "Bill, I am at peace BECAUSE I know that my son is in a beautiful place called heaven, which is so much better than this earth. I feel joyful and happy when I think about the wonderful reunion I will have there with my son someday. In the meantime, I am very thankful BECAUSE I have my husband and another son still with me. I want to be a positive and good wife and mother to them, and I know I can't do that with an eternal frown on my face."

Naturally, when I heard her words, I was moved by her story and inspired by her courage and how she was handling her tragic Lifeblow. Her choice to happen to life was as big as life. She was choosing her feelings, to be *happy* about her son being in heaven and *excited* about the reunion they would one day have. She was out of the darkness of her personal ground zero with the "new conversation": "*I choose ways I like to feel and find reasons in my life to feel <u>that</u> way.*"

She was also choosing many of the "new conversations" covered in this book. She was refocusing on the vision of a bright future with her husband and second son. She was present to her purpose as a loving mother and wife and knew why she wanted to be positive and productive every time she awakened to a new day. She had adopted an attitude of gratitude for the time she did have with her son and was grateful for the chance to spend time with the members of her family who remained. She was at the conference to receive support from positive influences and other victim's with a positive outlook, as I'll talk more about in the next chapter. I don't know of a better example of someone, who has taken such a negative experience and is directing their energy in such a worthwhile, meaningful, and extraordinary way.

Another wonderful example of our ability to choose our feelings can be seen in another mother who lost her son in the terrorist attacks. Todd Beamer's mom, whose son participated in overtaking the hijackers on the flight that crashed in Pennsylvania, exemplified her ability to choose in a TV interview after the attacks. She expressed how she was proud BECAUSE her son had the presence of mind in the midst of such chaos, even when he knew those were probably his final moments, to overtake the hijackers and thwart the attack. She said something like: "I feel good BECAUSE my son didn't die in vain when his courageous effort saved lives."

Todd Beamer AND his mother can be an inspiration to all of us. Todd, for his sacrifice and saving lives, and his mom for her example of furthering her healing process and experiencing fulfillment by choosing her feelings. You can also further your healing process and experience fulfillment with the "new conversation": *"I choose ways I like to feel and find reasons in my life to feel that way."*

ASK YOURSELF:

1. Where can I see I've been trapped with my attachment to unpleasant feelings — unable to experience other feelings for other people and things that would leave me fulfilled?

2. What reactive thoughts keep me attached to those unpleasant feelings?

3. After expressing those unpleasant feelings, what feelings do I choose to have going forward?

4. What perspectives can I embrace and get attached to as a result of choosing these feelings?

5. How can I complete the following sentence with ways I like to feel (i.e., happy, fulfilled, excited, peaceful, encouraged, fortunate, thankful, blessed, loved, appreciated, joyful)?

   I feel/am _____ because_____.
               (chosen feeling)   (reason to feel that way)

CHAPTER 15

WAY #9: SPEND TIME WITH THE RIGHT PEOPLE, AT THE RIGHT TIME

"I choose my discussions wisely."

O THER PEOPLE CAN HAVE AN ENORMOUS IMPACT ON OUR THOUGHTS and feelings, which, in turn, either lifts us up from our personal ground zero or keeps us stuck there; therefore, it's important to be aware of how we can be influenced by others in the aftermath of our Lifeblow.

This chapter is not about protecting ourselves from the criticism of others, but rather from another subtle threat that is also harmful and limiting; that is, when we get agreement from people around us for our reactive *truths*. Each time we get agreement for our harmful reactive *truths*, we silently affirm how very *RIGHT* we are about our reactive perspective. That's why other people's agreement isn't recognized as harmful. It occurs to us as support and often comes from people who love and care about us a great deal. This can create an interesting challenge for "Getting Up When Life Blows You Down." You momentarily feel good because you are being supported, but over the long haul, you stay chained to reactive conversations that keep you stuck at your personal ground zero. Breaking that chain requires starting the "new conversation":

I CHOOSE MY DISCUSSIONS WISELY.

For weeks after being released from the hospital, I regularly called the detective who was working on my case, to find out if the robber had been caught. Each time I was informed that he was still unaccounted for, I would hang up the phone, disappointed and upset, thinking about how unfair it would be if the robber got away with what he had done. Many people in my life knew how important it was for me to know that justice was prevailing. As a result, I got a tremendous amount of support for continuing to make the call to the detective. Each new day was another opportunity to pursue fulfillment by hoping my call would bring news of the robber being caught. In time, my persistence with that phone call diminished. The "new conversations" I had already made a part of my life, moved me onward and upward, as did my progress in the area of forgiveness, which I'll talk more about in chapter 17.

Even so, a few years later when I still had no idea if the robber had been caught, I'd sometimes find myself in conversations (about justice, the unfairness of life, and how I needed to keep checking on the robbers' status) that left me feeling lousy. On occasion, with one friend in particular, this conversation would even escalate to the point that he would suggest I become a bounty hunter and go find the robber myself. I found that idea to be absurd, yet sometimes after parting ways, I would catch myself slipping back into a complaint about injustice. One day I realized what I was doing to myself. Complaining about the robber not being caught was another way for me to stay anchored in the past. My conversation with my friend was a mental and emotional tether to my personal ground zero. Without even realizing, I had given my power to choose fulfillment, over to a conversation my friend wanted to have. I wasn't *"choosing my discussions wisely."*

Once I gained that clarity, I learned about the importance of choosing my direction by choosing the conversations I engaged in. Choosing discussions wisely requires paying attention to the role people play after your Lifeblow. Each person who loves us and cares about our well being will be helpful after any Lifeblow. Without question, we need people to support us where we are immediately after a Lifeblow, including the time that our reactive *truths* run rampant and consume our thinking. We need love, support, and a safe space to vent, express our thoughts and feelings, and experience our hurt. This process takes time, and we <u>must</u> take the time to complete it. The people who comfort and move you forward in the healing process are helpful at that stage; however, they may not be the best people to help you at the stage of creating fulfillment by supporting your "new conversations" and offering some *new truth* of their own. Since the stages overlap, this distinction can be very difficult.

There's a fine line between how we get needed support and are helped by people who have empathy, and how we are *hurt* by that empathy with too much agreement about our reactive TRUTHS. Too much agreement for our reactive TRUTHS makes it extremely difficult to start and hold "new conversations" that enable us to experience fulfillment.

After a Lifeblow, we also need love that is expressed by people supporting us in where we want to go — onward and upward from our personal ground zero. That kind of support requires the introduction of new perspectives and encouragement to adopt them — NOT continuous agreement with the reactive TRUTHS that keep us down. Accepting responsibility for surrounding ourselves with such support assures that we maintain our progress up after a Lifeblow. Uplifting NEW TRUTHS provide a solid foundation on which to stand, so we don't slip back into our reactive TRUTHS and back down the slippery slope into a life of complaint. We must distinguish how people impact how we think and feel, and maintain our sure footing on our journey up by starting the "new conversation": *"I choose my discussions wisely."*

The next time I caught myself backsliding in our discussion about the robber possibly being free, and how unjust that would be, I told my friend that I wasn't going to talk about it anymore. I told my friend that I hoped no one else was being hurt by the robber and that he had his life straightened out. I said it would be great if the robber was making a positive difference, regardless of whether he was in jail or free. My friend thought I had lost my mind. My words were very hard for him to hear — much less embrace as his own philosophy. He cared a great deal about me and wanted to support me in the very natural, automatic reactive thought process for getting revenge and righting a wrong. When he heard I wasn't interested in more discussion about that, my friends' reaction reminded me of an experience I had years ago at the North Carolina State Fair.

As I was waiting for friends to return with funnel cakes and foot-long sausage dogs smothered in onions, I was standing near an exhibit. A interesting looking character was barking an announcement that for fifty cents, all passers-by could see "Big Al, The Worlds Largest Hog." I dug in my pockets, found some change, paid the entrance fee, and ascended the steps. After reaching the top and stepping through a curtain, I peered over a wall and into his pen and heard myself say, "Holy cow!" Big Al was as big as a cow and I remember walking around his pen, shaking my head in amazement at the size of this creature. His head was as big as a standard-sized TV. A sign said he weighed 5000 pounds and regardless of whether or not that was true, this hog was absolutely enormous. Looking at Big Al was like looking at a Martian — I had never seen anything like him before. I came out from behind the curtain and descended the steps, still shaking my head in disbelief.

At that time, half-eaten funnel cakes and sausage dogs were arriving and I quickly told everyone about the best adult entertainment at the fair. I just kept saying over and over, "You all <u>have</u> to go see Big Al! You won't believe it." I had just become the biggest fan and spokesperson for "The World's Largest Hog," and my enthusiasm left everyone scrambling for their money. Moments later, I smiled from ear to ear as I watched my curious friends climb the stairs to take in the view. Although I couldn't see them behind that curtain, I could hear them oohing and aahing, and giggling in amazement. When they exited, the looks on their faces were priceless. Like me, they were wide-eyed, shaking their heads in wonder.

My friend had the same look when he heard my new perspective about the robber and my wish for him to be making a positive difference in the world, even if he had never been caught. He might as well have just seen a 5000-pound hog named Big Al. Sometimes our response and new perspective, occurs to people as an unbelievable freak of nature. Like Big Al, our response isn't the norm, particularly for people who haven't created fresh new perspectives after their Lifeblows. If someone hasn't ever seen a 5000-pound hog and you show them one with your new perspective, their reaction will be to shake their head in disbelief and wonder what planet you just arrived from. That's okay. *Your* life is the one at stake.

After standing firm in my commitment to only engage in uplifting discussions, my friend eventually stopped asking about the robber. He knew my new stand for my life when he heard my words — "What you think of me is none of my business." I never heard another word about righting a wrong by becoming a bounty hunter. He got very clear that I had no interest in plunging into my past frustration by awakening my reactive TRUTHS. Perhaps he got used to my 5000-pound hog or he may have even just quietly stayed convinced that I was nuts. In either case, I didn't care. Even if he thought I was nuts, I knew I was screwed to the right bolt because I was secure in my journey up. I felt better and didn't slide back into my reactive thinking. Remember that the mighty oak tree was once a little nut that held its ground. Being mighty in our journey of "Getting Up When Life Blows Us Down" is made possible by sometimes being a nut and always holding the "new conversation": *"I choose my discussions wisely."*

If we aren't careful, we will rise above our challenge about as quickly as the people around us expect us to. I've found that people's expectations of me, often mirror the expectations they have of themselves. If people aren't accepting NEW TRUTHS and creating fulfillment after their challenges, they don't expect you to react any differently. We all know people who have had Lifeblows and remain in a state of unhappiness for years. Their Lifeblow continues to happen to them and they have not created a life beyond the victim state. They are anchored in OLD TRUTHS and are stuck feeling lousy and producing reactionary outcomes that leave them unfulfilled. Some of those people might be your best friends. They may encourage continued discussions that take you further and further from the fulfilling life you seek, and they do it as an expression of their love and support.

In some cases, other people simply don't want you moving beyond your challenge. We've all heard the saying "Misery loves company." As you already know, giving up your need to be right is one of the hardest things we will ever do as human beings. Watching you move beyond your Lifeblow by giving up your need to be right is threatening. When someone watches you do that and take bold steps to create fulfillment, your example invites them to move forward and do the same thing. Resistance occurs because they feel confronted. They feel like they are on the hook to do that themselves. It's much easier for people to keep you in a mode of complaint than give up theirs. When people see you in a victim state, they know they are not alone and they feel better and justified to stay there themselves.

After your Lifeblow, when you are seeking comfort and support, a person like the one described above may initially be helpful, as you comfort one another by sheer virtue of the fact that you aren't alone in dealing with a Lifeblow. Depending on the nature of their challenge, you might even be served by seeing how your situation could be worse. Beyond that, you would not be served by a relationship with this person if you wallowed in your misery together. That kind of relationship, over time, would do more harm than good. It would keep you at your personal ground zero. Therefore, this kind of person is one with whom you would want to *"choose your discussions wisely."*

Other *people* don't keep you at your personal ground zero. Your reactive discussions with them do. E. E. Cummings described very well, the challenge of staying true to the new you who you become with your "new conversations" after a Lifeblow. He said, "To be nobody — but yourself — in a world which is doing its best, night and day, to make you everybody but yourself — means to fight the hardest battle which any human being can fight, and never stop fighting." If the people you spend time with are toxic and leave you feeling down in the dumps or worse about yourself and your challenge, you must put limits to your discussions with others by controlling the quality of them.

So how do you control the quality of your discussions? There are a few ways. When people aren't being supportive of your response — and your discussions with them keep you stuck in your complaints — you must do one of the following: You must either limit your association, you must specify what you are and are not going to talk about, OR you must let people know how they can better support you. You can always choose who you are going to spend your time with, as well as how, when, where, and for how long. When you do the above, you are taking action on the "new conversation": *"I choose my discussions wisely."*

Many loving hands were outstretched in the aftermath of my Lifeblow. Some were hands I could take hold of for comfort, but not all of those comforting hands were capable of pulling me up and out of my reactive state after the shooting. That's why I encourage you to pay close attention to the company you keep. We can surround ourselves with people who help us move beyond our circumstances, or we can surround ourselves with people who keep us in discussions that hold us down. We must find people who call us out of our reactive state. We must have people in our life who love us so much, that they not only provide a source of comfort, but also gently call us forward, upward, and onward. They do this by having empathy and not making us wrong for our reactions AND by reminding us to accept responsibility for our station in life and exercise our power to choose "new conversations" to create fulfillment in spite of our Lifeblow.

Consider the following example of such a person in my life. Several years ago, I was having lunch with a friend of mine whose name is Aedan. We had independently launched our professional speaking careers, and, before long, our discussion turned to the challenges of growing our businesses. I was telling her about my difficulties and how I continuously felt out of my comfort zone and was often unsure about whether I was doing what I needed to be successful. I went on and on, elaborating on every aspect of my business that caused me the most frustration.

Aedan sat there, patiently listening to my woes, nodding her head and assuring me that she understood where I was coming from because she was faced with the same challenges. When I finally finished my saga, she put her hand on my arm, looked me in the eye and said, "I understand, Bill. So, what are you going to do about it?" Immediately, I clearly saw how I was wallowing in my complaining, playing the victim, and wrapped up in how RIGHT I was about my difficult situation.

Our conversations and discussions with people are either wings that give us flight to create fulfillment, or a ball and chain that keep us tied to our unhealthy reactions. As an outsider looking in, Aedan noticed my destructive thoughts before I did. She didn't blame me for having them. My friend allowed me to express my thoughts and feelings, and then lovingly helped me own up to my reaction. With her help, I stopped reacting and started proactive thinking and planning for how to move forward. She led me to more constructive thinking and a more constructive conversation. That's the kind of relationship that helps us live more fulfilling lives. It's friends like Aedan who you want on your "rise above Lifeblows" team.

One of the best ways to choose our conversations wisely is by surrounding ourselves with people who have created uplifting NEW TRUTHS for themselves after Lifeblows and who will openly talk about them. One of the benefits of speaking professionally is that I have a chance to meet so many wonderful people — such as the lady at the victim's conference. I am continuously inspired, by people who share their stories of triumph over very difficult circumstances. Sometimes when I meet people, their Lifeblow is in the distant past; they've weathered the winds and storm and now bask in the glow of the beautiful day they have created.

On other occasions, the people I meet are smack dab in the middle of dealing with their Lifeblow. They are still in the middle of their storm, yet they're at peace. It's as if they are in the eye of their hurricane, windblown and tired, but there is an assuredness that when the winds howl again, they will be just fine because they are anchored in some very stable and positive "new conversations". Regardless of the timeliness or nature of their Lifeblow, whenever I meet such a person, I always let them know of the inspiring and uplifting impact they have on me.

People like this are the angels you want to find. **Hold the hands that comfort. Hang on for dear life to the hands that pull you up from your personal ground zero.** Those hands are attached to people who are a light to guide you out of your darkness. Many people would love to share how they made progress and overcame their negativity, especially if it helped you out of your unhealthy reactive place. Their hands are extended and they want to pull and lift you up. They see helping people like you as part of their mission. Someone at some point probably helped them, and they love passing along that gift. You won't be bothering them with your request for time.

Many of these people are a phone call away. Consider your family and friends and challenges they have had. Ask them who they might know as someone who would welcome your call. There are counselors, coaches, associations, and organizations whose sole purpose is to support people through their challenges.

If you can't find one of these groups, consider starting one yourself. Read books, attend seminars, and listen to tape programs that contain uplifting messages by people sharing their stories of triumph. Regardless of who they are or how you get their message, when the people with whom you spend time do your heart, mind, and spirit good, continue to associate or increase your association with them.

During the week after the terrorist attacks, we saw the supportive power that others can bring to our lives after a Lifeblow. The people of New York immediately began supporting one another in the midst of their tragedy. I remember the story about five women whose husbands were missing after the towers collapsed. Their husbands worked together and they were collectively gathering information from hospitals that may show their husbands' names on an admittance list. They had set up a call center in one of their homes to organize and combine their efforts and to be together when new information came in.

They had one another when they needed a shoulder to cry on. They took care of one another's children and took turns making meals for one another. I'm not sure if any of their husbands were ever found, but thankfully they had each other during this unbelievable time of need. Hopefully their comfort for one another then has continued today to include supporting one another by choosing to engage in non-reactive, new and uplifting conversations. Hopefully, you are engaging in those too, with a commitment to the "new conversation": *"I choose my discussions wisely."*

ASK YOURSELF:

1. Of the people I spend a lot of time with (inner circle of family and friends), who supports me by helping me experience my feelings and vent my reactive thoughts?
   • Of the people in my inner and outer circle, who can I confide in?
   • Who can I cry with and turn to without them trying to fix me?

2. Who helps me rise out of my personal ground zero with new perspectives and conversations? Who keeps me stuck in reactive conversations?

3. Depending on who the people are and what role they have been playing, what would work best to help me move forward?:
   • Stop associating, limiting my association, asking them to support me differently?

4. With whom do I want to start associating more?
   • Who inspires me?
   • Who brings out my potential?
   • Who encourages me by their example to be the best I can be?
   • Who believes in me?

5. Do I need some new people as part of my "rise above Lifeblows" team?
   • If so, what types of people do I need? (Funny, Optimistic, Supportive, Patient, etc)

6. What associations or support groups could I get involved with?

CHAPTER 16

WAY #10: SELFLESSLY GIVE AND ABUNDANTLY RECEIVE

"I give myself away in service to others."

ONE NIGHT WHILE WALKING TO A RESTAURANT WITH A FRIEND, WE met a man who was living on the street. Four hours later, the three of us walked out of the restaurant. That evening was the beginning of a friendship I have with a homeless man named Robert. We meet at various coffee shops and sometimes talk for hours — taking one another on a journey into our very different lives, experiences, and worlds. So much is different about us, yet much is the same. Without exception, we always see part of ourselves in one another. We laugh at stories, argue our perspectives, dream our dreams, and encourage one another in our pursuit of them. Since becoming friends, we've both grown an enormous amount as human beings. Robert is one of the greatest teachers I've ever had the privilege of being around.

One morning I picked him up to go get a cup of coffee. When he got in my car, I noticed that he didn't have his coat. It was February in North Carolina and cold outside, dipping into the twenties at night. The last time I had seen Robert, he had on his coat, and so I asked him where it was. He waved off my question and started asking about me and how I was doing. I didn't pick up the conversation with him, but instead asked again, "Before we talk about anything else, tell me, where is your coat?"

He looked at me and said: "Bill, you know how cold it was last night? Well, I was sitting on the sidewalk with this older guy and he was shaking like a leaf. He was so cold, I could hear his teeth chattering. I felt so sorry for him, so I gave him my coat."

I think if you had been looking at me, you would have seen my jaw drop. Here was a man, who had literally given the clothes off his back to help someone else in need. His clothes were all he owned, but he still gave them away. I had always heard the statement, "It's not what you give that matters. It's what you have left AFTER you've given." I now understood that statement like never before.

What compels a man to help another even when the giving is clothes off his back on a cold winter night? Here's a guy who is about as far down as one can get. He's got nowhere to go but a sidewalk. He's hurt, angry, unaccepted, downtrodden, lost, ignored, forgotten, desperate, cold, tired, and scared. His two most pressing questions in life are about where his next meal will come from and what to do next to survive life on the street. He's literally in a test of survival, but gives his coat away on a cold winter night. Maybe, just maybe, we can learn something valuable from him about "Getting Up When Life Blows Us Down."

Shirley Chisholm, former member of Congress said, "Service is the rent you pay for room on this earth." I like that idea, and would add that it pays for a room with a magnificent view. Get up when you're down by taking action on the "new conversation":

I GIVE MYSELF AWAY IN SERVICE TO OTHERS.

Our objective in internalizing the above conversation is to become a selflessly *GIVING* human being. That's a very difficult thing to do when, in the aftermath of our Lifeblow, we are being right about being wronged. When our life and routine have been turned upside down, our nature tells us "It is not our turn to give. It's our turn to receive things that will restore what we've lost or the things our Lifeblow has taken." Our feelings of being short-changed can be so strong that our only answer to any suggestion that we be *GIVING* at a time like this is a resolute, "*I don't think so!*"

That was my attitude, a great deal of the time, while I was in the hospital. I wanted the world and people in it, to be different — to give me more than it had when it delivered my Lifeblow. In fact, if you had asked me, "Bill, what would you like the world to be like?" — my answer was clear, *"I would like to be able to walk around without being paranoid about what might happen to me next. I want a world I can trust; where people help, respect, love, and care for one another."* I wanted a more caring and compassionate world, *without* being a more caring and compassionate human being. Today I recognize that our greatest source of fulfillment and strength when times get tough comes from the love, encouragement, support, and understanding that we receive from others. That kind of energy from people has the power to heal, and we open the floodgates of that healing power when we GIVE those things away. Realizing fulfillment after a Lifeblow is instant and automatic when we get out of our selfish frame of mind and live the "new conversation": *"I give myself away in service to others."*

John Webster expanded on the miracle produced by this "new conversation" when he said, "One of the most beautiful compensations of life is that no man can sincerely endeavor to help another person without, in turn, helping himself." He was talking about the gift of *GIVING*.

The following is a great little story about helping oneself, as a result of helping others. I read it in a publication called *Bits and Pieces:*

When Albert Einstein was on the faculty of Princeton University, a little girl used to stop in and see him nearly everyday. The girl's mother met Einstein one day while he was taking a walk and she asked if the little girl's visits bothered him. He answered her that they did not. "Well, what exactly do you all talk about?" — asked the mother. "Sometimes, we don't talk much at all," Einstein answered. "But, she brings me cookies and I help her with her arithmetic homework."

When we selflessly give, we abundantly receive things that bring us fulfillment — including help on our homework from masters and cookies from sweet little girls. I learned about this phenomenon toward the end of my hospital stay — when I was able to leave my room and wheel up and down the hall in a wheelchair. Each time I left my room, I visited other patients. After seeing less fortunate people, I had a shift in my heart and heard myself offering words of encouragement. My spirit of giving had been awakened.

Whenever I returned to my hospital room, I thought about my visits — the people, the conversations we had, their smiles and words of thanks — and wanted to do more. Consequently, I started noticing opportunities and other ways to give. One of the first things I noticed were flower arrangements and plants that had been given to me by my family and friends. A few of the arrangements had to be put under my bed because there wasn't any more room for them on the windowsill and tables. My giving spirit asked, "Why should they stay under the bed, out of the way, where they can't be appreciated?" There was no good answer, so we gave them away to other patients who didn't have that kind of cheer in their room, for whatever reason.

At some point during that process, I became aware of something very profound. Every time I returned to my hospital room, I felt better than I had before I left. Eventually I realized why. The simple gestures of visiting with, and giving flowers to, other patients brought many smiles to many faces. Smiles are contagious. The smiles they gave back to me, and their friendliness and words of encouragement all affected me the same way mine affected them. Although they would say our visits were a gift to them, they were also as big a gift to me. My days were brighter and more rewarding and meaningful. Time passed much more quickly. Patients I visited began stopping by my room to check on me. On more than one occasion, their timing was perfect. They lifted my spirits when I was down. What goes around, does indeed come around! I saw evidence of the kind, thoughtful, caring, compassionate, and encouraging world I previously wished was out there, but was sure didn't exist.

Ghandi said, "We must be the change we wish to see in the world." The uplifting that I experienced, was not the result of something that any of us did. It was the result of what happens in any space when a giving spirit is at work. When we selflessly give from our heart, without expecting anything in return, we receive comfort and fulfillment that's impossible to manipulate or contrive. Waves of fulfillment began flowing in my life when my selfishness stopped and I started being the change I wanted to see in the world. All made possible by the "new conversation": *"I give myself away in service to others."*

In chapter 9, I wrote about playing a game called <u>Accepting Responsibility For My Lifeblow</u>, in order to identify things to do differently in the future to prevent a repeat of a Lifeblow. I shared how one of my more impractical answers to the question — "What could I have done to prevent being shot?" was, *"I could have been volunteering my time with kids at risk. Had I done that, its possible that I could have been a positive role model for the robber in a way that might have made a difference in the choices he made in life."* Months later, that impractical answer led me to a conversation with a counselor, who worked with women at a shelter for victims of domestic violence. She informed me of a need for volunteers to spend time with the children at the shelter while their moms were in a group therapy session. She stated that male volunteers were particularly sought after because the kids needed positive male role models at this stage in their lives. I knew in my heart of hearts that I was being called to give my time to that effort and soon afterward, began volunteering.

The more time I spent with those children, the more I saw how easily influenced and conditioned children are by the events taking place around them and the people they look to for guidance. Many were lost, confused, angry and venting. Our activities and games were usually filled with smiles and laughter, but on occasion — yelling and aggression were the order of the evening. I got punched, slapped, cussed out, spat on, and bitten. The fighting at home had taught them much about how to get and maintain control in their own lives.

While volunteering, I often wondered if my energy and time were making any difference. Besides that, I hadn't signed on for putting up with such abuse, even if it was from children. A child's scratches bleed the same as any adult's. After one particularly ugly night, I had pretty much decided I wasn't going to return the following week. As I was leaving the shelter, one of the counselors pulled me aside and told me that the little girl who bit me that night, had paid me the ultimate compliment. I looked at her like she was crazy, before hearing her say, *"Bill, she wouldn't do that if she didn't know she was safe. You provided a 'safe place' for her tonight. She knew you weren't going to hit her back or hurt her in any way. She didn't know that when she was living at home."* I decided to return the next week. However, I still periodically questioned my sanity, as well as my impact as a role model making a positive difference. I kept returning on faith, but in my humanness, also wanted evidence that something good was happening. There were plenty of other things I could have been doing.

One night at the end of the evening when the mothers were reunited with their kids, one of the mothers walked up to me and asked, "Are you Bill?"

I answered, "Yes," and with a big smile, she looked at me said, *"Thank you, thank you, thank you so much."*

I had no idea what she was talking about. I got it, however, when she pulled her son Jeffrey to her side, patted him on the head, and said, *"He hasn't stopped talking about you and your time together all week long."* Jeffrey looked up at me with a big smile, and as I looked into his eyes, I saw a child who represented all children. I saw a child I once was, you once were, and the robber once was. I saw a young boy who was as easily influenced by a healthy environment as an unhealthy one. Suddenly, I had a totally understanding heart for the young man who shot me. If only his environment had been more supportive and loving. There was so much more possibility for his life as a positive contributor to the world, than I saw and he showed on the morning of September 28, 1988.

I returned to volunteer the following week and Jeffrey and his mother were gone — hopefully to another safe place. I never saw Jeffrey again, but the image of his face has never faded — and I clearly know why. The moment of truth when our eyes met the last time we saw one another was not about anything I gave to Jeffrey. It was about what he gave to me. Jeffrey gave me understanding. He reminded me that each of us needs all of us and all of us need each of us along our journey of reaching our God-given potential. Jeffrey showed me *his* and *my own* infinite value, as well as that of the robber. He touched my heart, fed my soul, and lifted my spirits — all the result of seriously playing a game called <u>Accepting Responsibility For My Lifeblow</u> and living the "new conversation": *"I give myself away in service to others."*

David Dunn, in his book *Try Giving Yourself Away*, described my experience best, when he said — *"I've come to believe that my hobby of helping, of giving away, with the flush of pleasure it brings, is the finest heart tonic in the world."* Dunn hit the mark in describing the magic of abundantly receiving by giving ourselves in service to others, while expecting nothing in return. He also hit on another interesting fact to consider — GIVING of yourself to help others, is a powerful contributor to health and long life. Studies have revealed that people who did volunteer work at least once/week, outlived those who did none, nearly three-to-one. GIVING does your heart good in more ways than one. Your heart tonic is waiting in the "new conversation": *"I give myself away in service to others."*

For years after being shot, I had no intention to ever share my message as a professional speaker. I knew how my experience was a gift, even though it came wrapped in newspaper headlines and a lengthy hospital stay. The gift was the opportunity to grow as a human being as a result of my Lifeblow, but I never thought of the insights as something to share in the spirit of giving. It was not until I began sharing my story and some of what I had learned from my experience, and started receiving positive feedback, that I began to understand how our suffering can awaken our giving spirit, inspire a new purpose for our lives, and take on a whole new meaning as the basis of a spiritual practice to serve others.

My speaking business has been a vehicle for fulfilling that purpose. Naturally, writing this book is another way to fulfill it. I never imagined myself as an author, until it became another way to purposely serve. Regardless of the path that brought me where I am today, doing what I do in the spirit of giving has added more fulfillment to my life than I could ever have imagined. Your newfound wisdom, growth, and positive energy you've gleaned from your Lifeblow can inspire a new purpose and be shared with others in the same way. **The new and improved creation you have become since your Lifeblow, with what you have learned about life and being your best in it, is a GIFT that you can give other people.** In the words of Angela Davis, "We must learn to lift as we climb."

The lady whose son was murdered, whom I mentioned in chapter 14, did that. While we were talking, she also shared how giving herself away in service to others, had helped her find fulfillment in spite of her Lifeblow. Not only is she committed to give of herself to her husband and second son, she found another compelling purpose and way to *GIVE* in light of her tragedy. She told me: "Even though my son is dead, since I'm still here I figure there must be something God wants me to do with the time I have left on this earth. Today, I know what that is — it's why I'm at this conference. My purpose is to give of myself to fight for victim's rights. By doing that, maybe what happened to my son and our family won't happen to somebody else and theirs." She was giving herself away to a worthy cause that helped other people. It was in her GIVING to a passionate cause, that she found some of the greatest heart tonic in the world.

In the words of Ruth Smeltzer, "You have not lived a perfect day, even though you have earned your money, unless you have done something for someone who will never be able to repay you." To me, that quote contains a great definition of selfless giving that really gets the heart tonic flowing. A great example can be seen in Percy Ross — a millionaire-turned philanthropist who doled out millions of cash to readers of his syndicated column, "Thanks A Million" which appeared in 800 newspapers for sixteen years. He died at age eighty-four after giving away an estimated $30 million for everything from organ transplants to the building of recreation centers. In a farewell column he wrote in 1999, he told his readers, "I've achieved my goal. I've given it all away. You've given me so much over the years. In many respects, I'm far richer today than when I started." Percy Ross showed how we can multiply happiness by dividing it.

Richard Bach said, "Here's a test to find whether your mission on earth is finished: if you're alive, it isn't." Percy Ross and the lady who lost her son, made *GIVING* a part of their life's mission, and received the reward of fulfillment as a result. What you can do in the spirit of GIVING is endless. You don't have to give away $30 million to grow richer. You can give of yourself and help others with such simple gestures as a smile, opening a door, helping with groceries, or doing a favor. You can give of yourself by writing a note, sending a card, giving a compliment, recognizing someone for an accomplishment, sending a gift, or holding an elevator a little longer for a complete stranger.

Volunteering is a wonderful option too. You can spend your time at a hospital for the terminally ill, a shelter for abused and neglected people, feeding the homeless and elderly, taking care of people who are mentally or physically disabled, or caring for animals without a home. Whether it's visiting residents in a nursing home or babysitting for neighbors so they have a chance to spend an evening alone, you climb into bed with a smile on your face. The heart tonic tastes good and is refreshing, because you're living the "new conversation": *"I give myself away in service to others."*

After the terrorist attacks, we saw the *giving spirit* inherent in ourselves and every human being on the planet. Most of us heard about the selfless giving of people helping one another out of the World Trade Center, including the two guys who carried a woman in a wheelchair down ninety flights of stairs to safety. We saw selfless giving in the man who owned a shoe store near Ground Zero. As people ran away from the collapsing World Trade Center, he was giving away tennis shoes to help people wearing dress shoes or high heels, run faster. We saw this giving spirit in the heroic actions of those involved in rescue efforts, working to exhaustion day and night.

We also saw our spirit of selfless giving in long lines at blood donation centers, where hundreds of people waited in line for hours to do something to help. We saw it in the way people shared other talents, such as counseling skills to help others with their grief and ability to cope. My favorite example being that of Melanie Sovern, a ten-year-old girl whose mother died of breast cancer when Melanie was five. At the time I am writing this, she is giving her time to kids who lost a parent in the attacks — sharing her message that they can still have a good life, that they can still experience fulfillment in spite of their Lifeblow.

One unnamed man, who lost his wife and daughter in the attacks, started a Foundation of Tolerance and Understanding at his daughter's school. In spite of enormous losses — he found heart tonic in giving back to his community and making a positive difference in the lives of other children and future of our country.

We've seen our spirit of selfless giving and its healing impact in the letters that thousands of people took time to write and send to NYC firemen. One spoke of the impact those cards and letters have had on his ladder company in supporting and encouraging them as the recovery and healing process continued. He said, *"On break you just look through a stack of cards from people, from school kids, from everyone — and it gives you the little boost you need to get through another day."* The firemen who give and give of themselves in service to others are getting back the love that helps them heal. What goes around, does indeed come around.

A spirit of giving saved lives, lifted people up, gave people hope, and helped our country rise out of the ashes of tragedy. In a multitude of expressions, our spirit of selfless giving, to a purpose greater than ourselves, was awakened — and it felt good. The roots of happiness and fulfillment indeed grow deepest in soils of service and the "new conversation": *"I give myself away in service to others."*

Og Mandino, in his book *A Better Way To Live*, poses a powerful question: "What if you begin treating everyone you meet — your family, your neighbors, your coworkers, strangers, customers, even enemies if you have any, as if you knew a deep, dark secret about each of them. The secret: that they, along with you, are living their last day on this earth and will be dead by midnight! Now, how do you suppose you would treat everyone you meet today, if you knew they would be gone forever at day's end? You know how. With more consideration and care and tenderness and love than you ever have before. And how do you suppose they would respond to your kindness? Of course! With more consideration and kindness and love and cooperation than you ever experienced from others in the past."

We all learned from the terrorist attacks that we could be dead by midnight, and selfless giving flowed out of that perspective. Our nation began healing and being uplifted because we started *GIVING* and *RECEIVING!* If all of us could just remember that and apply it on a daily basis — particularly after Lifeblows.

One way I remind myself that SELFLESS GIVING is a choice with a priceless reward, is to read the message on the opposite page. I wrote this message to help me notice and stop everyday little unhealthy reactions that steal my now moment happiness and fulfillment. Inspired by my gift of being shot, I call it my ATM CARD, an acronym for "Appreciate This Moment, Choose A Rewarding Day."

The choice is yours. There are at least five things you can do with your hands after a Lifeblow. You can wring them in despair, fold them in helplessness, clinch them in anger, hold them up in surrender, or use them to help someone.

Much of the world is on the wrong scent in pursuit of fulfillment and happiness. They think it consists of having, getting, accumulating and being served by others. If only they knew the secret of a homeless man, sitting on a sidewalk in the dead of winter without his coat.

My homeless friend, Robert, gave his coat for the same reason firemen give their exhaustive effort and the rest of us give our blood, money, encouraging words, expertise, love, time, and tennis shoes to those less fortunate. **Selfless giving is a heart tonic, served up on a higher road that leads out of the darkness at personal ground zeros and into the light of fulfillment.** Don't delay the joy you'll get from giving and receiving. Drink up and fill your head with the "new conversation" — *"I give myself away in service to others."* — and don't be surprised when your heart gets filled because you did.

Appreciate This Moment, Choose A Rewarding Day

Today is a gift from God. The chance to live another day.
This moment is important. It's the only one I'm guaranteed.
This moment is significant. Only I choose how to fill it.
This moment is profound. It will never be seen again, but its effects
will be.
My words and actions are my contribution to a world,
Standing open armed like a child, hoping for the positive difference
I CAN make.
As I pass through this moment, my greatest reward in living
Lies not in the "CAN I?" but rather in the "WILL I?"

ASK YOURSELF:

1. Where/for whom am I giving of my time, talents, energy, and/or gifts, in a way that makes a positive difference and where I have no thoughts of self gain?

2. If currently not giving of myself, how could I do so in service to others?

3. When am I going to start?

4. Am I supporting other people the same helpful ways I've been supported?

5. Where could I be volunteering or share my lessons and growth as a gift to others?

CHAPTER 17

WAY #11: CHOOSE GOD

SOME PEOPLE HAVE QUESTIONED MY APPROACH TO DEALING WITH challenges — for noticing harmful reactions, stopping them, and starting "new conversations" to create fulfillment after a Lifeblow — stating that it leaves little, if any, room for turning to God when times get tough; that turning our hearts and minds to God is a better way up from a personal ground zero. One woman felt concerned that "new conversations" would lead her away from God.

The following question was within a letter I received after a speaking appearance:

> Bill, I do have a question that has caused me some difficulty with most if not all PMA (Positive Mental Attitude) philosophies and the question is this: "Does God have a place in a person's life who has developed highly successful PMA skills?" It seems to me that once you have honed your skills, really perfected them, that your need to call on a higher power would be lessened and ultimately there would be few, if any, situations that you in your power, wouldn't be able to process your way out of. Have you found that to be the case?

For me, getting shot at the ATM was a benchmark. I began questioning how God was working in my life. Since that time I've grown considerably in my faith and gained additional understanding about how God is working, the kind of person God wants me to be and how to be that kind of person. As my relationship with God has developed, I have found God to be the source of ALL that enables us to "Get Up When Life Blows Us Down." It is from that perspective that I answer questions such as those posed in the letter I received in 1997.

QUESTION: Does mastering the process I outline in this book, leave little or no room for God in my life?

NO.

QUESTION: Does mastering this process shut God out as a source of strength and comfort when I'm at a personal ground zero?

ABSOLUTELY NOT.

QUESTION: Does mastering this process, lessen my need to call on God to help me through challenging times? Does it make me self-dependent instead of God-dependent?

HEAVENS NO!

At the time of the shooting, I had been attending church and Sunday school for many years. I had listened to sermons, prayed daily and heard about Godly principles and how to apply those principles to everyday living. I knew when I prayed that God could hear me, which was comforting, but my communication with God was always one-way. As I said my prayers, God always occurred to me as way out there somewhere. I was on earth and God was in some very faraway place above the clouds in a place called heaven. As I look back on my life at the time of the shooting, I knew a lot ABOUT God.

After getting shot, I began to develop a new kind of relationship with God. I began to experience God in a brand new way, later recognizing that God's presence was and is WITH me, just as a friend might be with me at a ball game, while eating lunch, or on a business appointment. I learned that God is not out there somewhere far, far away, but rather right here — right now — ALL the time. I learned we have two-way communication, where we can talk to God and also hear from God. That began my journey of really KNOWING God instead of just knowing ABOUT God.

My friend Bonny remembers walking with her father as a child. She remembers how her father's large hand would hang near her shoulder and sometimes she'd reach up and grab one of his big thick fingers as they walked. On occasions, she would leave her father's side and venture out to pick a flower, chase a butterfly, climb a tree, or play in a puddle. Sometimes she would return with a big smile, holding a flower she picked for her mom or telling her story of chasing a butterfly. Sometimes, her choices to explore and discover were painful or embarrassing. The smiles might become tears if she was hurt from a thorn pricking her finger or a scraped knee resulting from a tree branch that wouldn't hold her; however, if she did get hurt, my friend knew just what to do. Her father was ALWAYS standing there with outstretched arm, extended hand, and dangling finger — waiting for her to return to his side and grab hold for comfort.

Our life and walk with God is a lot like that. God has been with us from the beginning of our miraculous creation. He created us in his image. God is LOVE. God is all that accompanies and encompasses LOVE — joy, peace, trust, acceptance, patience, forgiveness, kindness, caring, giving, compassion, and gentleness. We were created that way. We are ONE with God.

We can see evidence of our being created in God's image in the innocence of babies and very young children. I was standing in line at the bank not long ago and watched two little girls, of different cultures, playfully peeking at each other and giggling as they took turns peering at one another from behind their mothers' legs. They were having a ball! They were happy, trusting, friendly, accepting, loving, and playful. Within a few minutes, they left their mothers' legs and moved closer to one another, reaching out to touch hands in a very innocent and unconditionally accepting way. There was no doubt while watching them giggle and get acquainted, that they could have spent the entire day together in perfect bliss. As I watched them, it was impossible for me not to smile.

Suddenly, both mothers spoke, almost simultaneously, calling their children's names in an authoritative manner before grabbing them and returning them to their sides. The children were surprised, but within a few seconds, started their dance all over again. They never got close enough to touch again, as the line moved along and eventually one of the mothers was called forward by the teller. The entire time the mothers made their transactions, the smiling and waving never stopped and it wasn't until the first girl and her mother actually left the building that this new relationship came to an end.

One thing I noticed that day while standing in line was that the two mothers never looked at one another. They never made eye contact or even acknowledged one another's presence or the magic of the encounter their children were having.

There was a dramatic difference between those children and their mothers. Over the years, society had influenced the mothers' beliefs, in a way that prevented them from being so freely expressed, accepting, open, and friendly as their children. They, like most adults, were afraid of being so naturally and lovingly related to one another. Their reaction that day in the bank spoke volumes about how all of us get conditioned. Perhaps somewhere along the way, "Don't speak to strangers," took on a whole new meaning as an overall better way to live. Whatever happened, the beliefs of those mothers left each of them unable to allow the beautiful encounter of their children to continue, and ultimately guided the actions they took to separate them.

What a huge contrast there is, between the fear and skepticism we have toward one another as adults, and the unconditional love and acceptance of children. When Queen Rania of Jordan was interviewed on CNN about the terrorist attacks, she shared how her son, after watching TV coverage, asked, "Why would people do that to other people they don't even know?"

Children have no biases, beliefs, prejudices, or political points of view. With regard to terrorist attacks, adults ask *why* because it is difficult for us to *understand* how people could be so cruel and have no value for human life. Innocent children ask *why* because they don't *know* there is any other way, outside of acceptance and love, to treat fellow human beings.

Somewhere in all the learning, living, and conditioning since the time we were just babes behind the nursery window, we lost touch with the magnificence of being so friendly, free, loving and fully related to one another. Evidence of this is readily seen when adults who don't know one another, are standing in an elevator. Everyone is looking up, almost anxiously waiting for the doors to open to disrupt the uncomfortable silence and move on in their separate worlds. Young children never act that way in elevators.

As human beings, we start out as unconditionally loving children and become very conditional in our acceptance of one another as adults. The difference between human beings and God is that God's way never changes. God is always, always, always, in every moment of every day — unconditional love. We don't have to worry, speculate, figure out, or guess how God might be today — how God might feel about us or act toward us. God is the same today as he was yesterday and will be tomorrow. God just IS unconditional love, all of the time.

Since our relationship with God and experience of God have nothing to do with who God is being, let's look at what impacts if or how much we *realize* God. When we have a Lifeblow and our natural human reaction is anger, frustration, and anxiety, we often wind up sabotaging many of the things we value and cherish, such as significant relationships and our health. When we create a life that we truly don't enjoy, more negativity and discord are generated, and our reward is often the creation of more negative circumstances. The cycle is a vicious one, and we suffer the consequences — a life that is empty, unfulfilling, unfruitful, and barren. We pay the price of misery for a life worth complaining about.

Our suffering is not brought on by God. Our suffering is brought on by ourselves in letting our human negativity run rampant. Peace after Lifeblows can only be found when we return to where our home is and always has been —within ourselves in the place called our soul. It is there that our spirit resides. It is there that our connection to God as our source of strength and peace, is, and always has been. That place inside is all that was when we were born, but it got covered up with conditioning and buildup of ego and human reactive ways. Our true nature is underneath all of that, and we lose touch with it. In being out of touch with our essence, we're not open, giving, compassionate, grateful, understanding, trusting, patient, or unconditionally loving. We're not at peace. We're not present. We just want to get off the elevator.

Our harmful reactions have taken us further and further from God and all that we need to be uplifted. In the midst of our complaint about life at our personal ground zero we forget, or fail to realize, that our greatest source of comfort is unfailingly standing by, no matter what, no matter how long we've been away. God's loving and accepting hand is always outstretched, waiting patiently for us to return, to take hold and experience the peace that comes when we walk with God.

So how do we reestablish our connection? As creatures in God's image we also have the capacity to create our lives with our thoughts, words, and actions. God said, "Let there be light," and there was light. God spoke and it was created. Everything God created was brought into existence with words. When we were born in God's image, we got the same power in a gift called *choice*. We create our lives with the words we choose.

For instance, we can choose the words we speak to another person. Depending on the words we use, we create our life experience. If my words are respectful and uplifting, I create harmony. If my words are offensive and disrespectful, I create conflict. Let's say a waitress brings us a wrong food order. We can look at her like she's an idiot and say something nasty or we can provide a gentle reminder. Being nice may improve our service the rest of the way. Being nice may even make our food taste better. After all, until it is served she has control of what goes in it! We create our life experience with our words.

We can also choose the internal words we use, our thoughts. As we have already covered, these words create our lives and results by the way they impact how we feel and what we do. Since our reactive thoughts often create circumstances we complain about, God gave us the power to choose. He gave us that power because He loves us. Since He created us from love and as love, He wants us to create our lives in this world and interact with His other children in the world, with love. We reestablish our connection to God when we use our gift of choice to stop our reaction and respond and be who we really are — a loving creation. Choosing to live in such a way is simply using the gift God gave us to live the way he brought us into the world.

One day a farmer was out in his field, tending to a spectacular crop that was ready to be harvested. While pausing for a drink of water near a roadside fence, the farmer noticed a car pull to the side of the road. He turned to see a minister stepping from the car, so he waved and said, "Good afternoon." The minister waved back, then crossed the road and walked up to the fence.

They shook hands and the minister said, "My goodness, you have an absolutely beautiful field of crops. I couldn't help but notice as I drove by, and I immediately felt the need to stop and tell you how beautiful the view is from the road."

The farmer smiled and said, "Well, thank you. Before you stopped, I was admiring the view as well."

The minister then commented, "God is so good. You do realize that none of what we are both admiring, would be possible without God?"

The farmer smiled again and said, "You are so right. You know I have really been blessed this year, and I am so very thankful. None of this would be possible without God. God truly is great and good."

The minister nodded approvingly and responded, "I just wanted to make sure you were giving credit where credit is due."

With that being said, the minister once again shook the farmer's hand, let him know he was very pleased that the farmer knew God's work when he saw it, wished him well, and turned to walk back to his car.

The farmer watched the minister cross the road and just as the minister opened the door to climb behind the wheel, the farmer called out and said, "Excuse me sir."

The minister turned to see the farmer giving a broad gesture toward the field and then heard the farmer say, "God is great and God is good, and none of this is possible without him. With regard to this field of crops, however, you should have seen this place when He had it all to Himself."

This story reminds me of how our lives parallel that of the farmer's. The beautiful field of crops was created by using God's gift (seeds); however, the farmer had to do his part. None of this beautiful new creation could have been created without God's gift and the farmer's effort to use it properly. We are like the farmer and the field of crops is like our life.

Just as the farmer had to have a <u>desire to create</u> new life (the crop),

SO MUST WE.

Just as the farmer had to <u>use God's gift</u> of seed to create new life,

SO MUST WE USE GOD'S GIFT OF CHOICE.

Just as the farmer had to <u>have faith</u> that using God's gift would yield new life,

*SO MUST WE HAVE FAITH THAT MAKING NEW CHOICES WILL
YIELD A NEW AND BETTER LIFE.*

Just as the farmer had to <u>bring his effort, commitment, dedication, and persistency</u> to the process of plowing the field and planting and nurturing the seed, in order to reap the rewards,

*SO MUST WE BRING OUR COMMITMENT & EFFORT TO
NOTICING OUR REACTIONS, STOPPING THEM, CHOOSING
"NEW CONVERSATIONS," AND NURTURING OUR NEW WAY
OF THINKING.*

We must use our minds and make certain choices if we want to grow in our relationship with God and be ONE with God. One Bible verse that calls us forth in that way, is Romans 12:2, saying "And do not be conformed to this world, but be transformed by the renewing of your mind." Regardless of your religious persuasion or spiritual orientation, I know that God didn't create any of us walking around with a chip on our shoulder, beating ourselves up, constantly feeling angry and disgruntled and miserable and treating others accordingly.

I know God didn't create me to NOT speak to my parents and not allow friends to share their love because I'm fantasizing about beating someone with a baseball bat. When our unhealthy reactions continue unchecked and we don't exercise our ability to choose and renew our mind and transform our life, we stay stuck and separated from the kind of person God created and intended us to be. When we use God's gift of CHOICE to create a more fulfilling life, we delight in God's will. When each "new conversation" lifts us up to experience more peace and joy so that we can love and contribute positively to one another, we return to God's side, we take God's hand, and we walk in God's ways. Peace is our reward because we are connected to the source of all good things. We have not processed our way through our Lifeblow without depending on God. We have depended fully on God and God's gift of choice to be freed from our life of complaint.

When we live in love, unhealthy reactions take a road trip. When love is present, anger vanishes, fear runs away, frustration gives up, discouragement retreats, disappointment dies, depression looks up, distrust trusts again, helplessness gains strength, despair disintegrates, resentment forgives, self pity accepts responsibility, and idleness springs into action to cause and create fulfillment. When we exercise our choice to produce those outcomes with our words ("new conversations"), we honor God. We glorify God. We lift our hearts to God. We put ourselves in God's hands. However you want to say it, fulfillment comes because we CHOOSE GOD.

CHOOSE GOD WITH THE NATURE OF YOUR PRAYER

I've described the shock and disbelief I felt after being shot. I could not believe that this had actually happened to me, partly because of what I knew ABOUT God. For years I had heard that "God is love," and "everything happens for a reason." My interpretation of these sentiments was that God is ultimately lovingly involved in everything that happens to us. He loves us that much. Because I had never thought about that statement in any great depth, I never questioned that idea ABOUT God and how God works in our lives. It always sounded very encouraging to me — that God lovingly is orchestrating everything that happens to fulfill a higher purpose.

After being shot, all of that changed. Applying that idea to my experience at the ATM was completely unsettling. How in the world could a loving God, orchestrate my being shot? Why would a loving God do that? If this experience was from God, allowed by God, what else was going to happen to me? I was at a complete loss — losing faith, losing hope, losing peace, and losing my mind. I felt afraid and worried and anxious. I was confused and felt horrible. My inner turmoil led me to start a new kind of conversation with God.

This conversation was unlike any I had ever had with God before. It wasn't a prayer for the safety of my family or giving thanks for a meal I was about to eat. Instead, it was a question, a very demanding question, *"WHY ME!?" God, why would you do this? Why would you allow it? What have I done wrong?"* It was an angry prayer. I was blaming God. I was making God wrong and the target of my anger and upset. I was relating to God as someone I couldn't trust. I wasn't taking God's hand. I was pushing God away, and making it impossible to experience God's presence, peace, love, comfort, and strength.

One time I started one of my speeches with the very strong statement, "If there is one word that has more to do with how your life is going to turn out, than any other word, THAT word is ATTITUDE."

Immediately, a man in the audience yelled, "What about God?"

I invited him to discuss that with me after my speech, and at that time, shared that the premise: "If there's one word that has more to do with how our life is going to turn out, than any other word, THAT word is attitude," includes our attitude toward God. Our attitude can keep us separated from God and unable to experience God's presence.

The wonderful thing about God and God's way never changing is that we can push God away, but God never *goes* away. I learned that God does acknowledge our angry prayers. (Angry prayers are better than no prayers at all. After all, if we didn't believe that God is good, we could never be mad at God.) Even if our prayer is a resentful, "Why me?," if we are truly seeking understanding, God will lead us to the answer and back to a godly way of being — where we experience fulfillment and peace.

Over time, the nature of my prayers began to shift. The words didn't change. I still prayed, "Why me?" but gradually did so with less and less anger. I stopped blaming God and simply asked the same question, "Why me?" with a different attitude. I asked the question as a student would ask a mentor. I was confused and I really wanted to understand. My new attitude turned my prayer into a genuine question for guidance. In fact, in a short time, my prayer "Why me?" expanded to the prayer "Father, guide me. Help me understand."

I had never before inquired into how God was working in my

life. I had never asked God to help me understand anything. I had heard the phrase, "seek and ye shall find," but had never interacted with God to find anything. I learned through praying, "Father, guide me," that faith gets ignited and hope flows forth because we have asked God into our lives to help us through our challenge. We've actually made room for God to work in us because we have gotten our reactive self, out of the way.

When we are praying for guidance, hearing God requires that we quiet the noisy reactive thoughts about our Lifeblow. There is a direct correlation between how much of God's guidance we actually notice, and how full our head is of reactive thoughts. When my prayer "Why me?" held more of a spirit of anger and blame, I was not fully open to hear God. My head was busy with and full of the noise of my reactive thoughts. When that is the case, God's guidance might be there, but we miss it.

A good example would be the following scenario: Suppose I want to get out of an unfamiliar building and have asked you to help guide me. You could be standing near a door and pointing in the direction I need to go, but if I'm looking out the window and preoccupied in my thoughts, I'll miss your guidance. It's there, but I'll miss it because my focus is away from you.

This can happen when we ask for God's guidance. The guidance may come very quickly; God is holding the door open for us to walk through, but we might not recognize it because our reactive thoughts have our attention focused elsewhere.

When my prayer shifted to seek more understanding, and I quieted my reactive thoughts, I was more open and able to hear God. Psalms 46:10 says, "Be still and know that I am God." To hear God's guidance, we must get quiet and get our reactive selves out of the way. We can do that by taking a walk in nature, working out, or sitting in a quiet sanctuary. We can do it through prayer and meditation, anywhere at anytime. Today, my prayers for guidance always include, "Help me recognize Your guidance when You deliver it." When our reactive thoughts settle down, and we quiet the noise in our heads, we can slide by our big reactive brain and hear God's voice.

After getting my reactive self out of the way, little did I know I was about to experience God on a level that would bring an entirely new meaning to my life. A major turning point for me occurred one day when God answered my prayer. For the first time in my life, I learned that when we ask God to be part of our lives, God immediately enters in and directs a path to fulfillment, joy, and peace.

That happened for me when God gave me a book. He delivered it to me in the hands of my dad and it was the first time I became aware that God's presence is not in some faraway place, way out there somewhere I can't see or touch. God's presence is right here, right now, and can be experienced in the outflow of love we receive from others. Our unconditional love as humans, IS God's love. Where our unconditional love is, God is. When that comes from someone who is standing or sitting beside us, God is in that space. The book I was given is called, *When Bad Things Happen To Good People*, written by Rabbi Harold Kushner, and it contained answers to my prayer, "Help me understand."

Kushner's book reminded me that I had a "say" in the matter of my life — that I can choose and am choosing all the time. It offered me a new perspective about being shot. A perspective that would play a significant role for me in "Getting Up When Life Blew Me Down." This perspective would also help me to grow in my faith and desire to be more ONE with God, more often. God wasn't punishing me at the ATM. He wasn't getting my attention for messing up or doing something wrong. God did NOT orchestrate or allow the shooting so that I would experience enough pain and anguish to get motivated to get my act together. We don't have to work for God's love. God loves us unconditionally.

In giving us the gift of choice, in creating us in his image, God doesn't dictate what we choose, or our ability to choose would be pointless. Choice wouldn't be an option. We'd be like a cow, or a beetle, or a kangaroo, or a zebra. God gave us the gift of choice, and we can choose to stay connected to him — or not. God simply allows us to exercise our gift. All human beings are choosing all the time. On September 28, 1988, I chose to wake up at 3:30 AM. I chose to get out of bed, take a shower, and get dressed for work. I chose to eat a bagel for breakfast instead of a bowl of cereal. I chose to stop at the ATM on my way out of town. My being at the ATM was my choice, and I happened to make that choice at the same time another human being was choosing to be there for a very different reason. I got shot because two human beings made choices about how to live their life that day. The robber and I could have said "NO" to being at the ATM just as easily as we said, "YES." That realization and understanding provided an opening for me to really begin building a stronger relationship with God. My getting shot happened for a reason, just as getting married and getting laid off or getting a dream job — happen for the same reason —to provide a new opening and opportunity to build a stronger relationship with God.

Once I knew I didn't have to be afraid of what God was going to do to me next, my prayer matured and the words "Guide me" took on further meaning. Instead of *"Guide me. Help me understand,"* my prayer became *"Guide me. I trust you. This is a tough deal. Help me to get through it. Please give me the strength and courage to handle this challenge with grace."* With that simple shift in my conversation with God, anger and fear slipped away and peace entered in — instantly, effortlessly, painlessly, and naturally. That's what happens when we take God's hand, ask God into our life, and become ONE with the source of all good things.

With my prayer, "Guide me," I got guidance to not only accept responsibility for my choices on the morning I was shot, but also for choices that were contributing to my miserable existence in the hospital. That is when I began noticing the opportunity to make additional attitudinal shifts and start "new conversations" in the hospital. I crashed my pity party with the new perspectives I've shared in this book, all of which were continued steps along my journey of being uplifted after my Lifeblow. Many people are praying for mountains of difficulty to be removed, so they can find happiness again — instead of praying for guidance, strength, and courage to climb them happily.

After our Lifeblow we can either pray, *"Why me?"* with a blaming attitude, where we seek no understanding and distance ourselves from God as our source of comfort. On the other hand, we can pray, *"Guide me,"* and ask God to be present in our life to lead us and give us strength and courage to rise out of our personal ground zero. *"Why me?"* as I was praying initially, is a prayer based in fear. *"Guide me"* is a prayer that is based in faith. Choosing the nature of our prayer is choosing to be God-loving or God-fearing, to walk with God or to be separated from God. Being God's miracles, we weren't created by

Him to live our lives in fear. God doesn't smile when we are full of anxiety, doubt, and worry that grow out of being afraid. At the miracle of our creation, we were brought into being with only love. Fear is learned. We learn fear through human conditioning, over time, as we grow older. Again, consider babies and young children. They are fearless. A baby isn't afraid of moving to a new city. A baby isn't afraid of what someone else might think of them. A baby isn't afraid of being abandoned or losing a loved one. A baby isn't afraid of dying. A baby isn't afraid of being kissed by a stranger. A baby isn't afraid of being held and cradled and adored in the arms of an intoxicated homeless person.

Let us learn much from the babies. God created us free of fear and full of love and wants us to live that way. When I was afraid of what God might do to me next, I didn't trust my relationship with God. I had no desire to reach out to God when I saw him as the source of my current pain, as well as more pain down the road. By positioning God as my adversary, I blocked myself from experiencing the peace and fulfillment that is guaranteed when we are God-loving and take God's hand and walk with God after a Lifeblow.

God has not given us a spirit of FEAR toward Him and others, but of FAITH and LOVE. Fear doesn't serve us when it creates separateness and avoidance from the source of our healing. That's what happened to me when I was afraid of what God might do to me next. I avoided being closer. My fear separated me from God. Fear led me further from faith, further from love, further from trust, and further from all I needed to rise above my personal ground zero.

You may have heard the very short story — FEAR knocked. FAITH answered and NO one was there. Fear disappeared because it cannot exist in the same space as faith. In any given moment, I can either fear God or have faith in God, but I can't do both — not at the same time. When fear blocks our ability to live a full life and reach our God-given potential, God isn't smiling at the wonderfully limited life we've created.

Our loving God has given us all we need to experience fulfillment after any Lifeblow — the gift of *choice*. Too often, we forget to use that gift. We often forget that we even have it. We are so much like the characters in the movie, *The Wizard of Oz*. Dorothy, the Lion, the

Tinman, and the Scarecrow were unfulfilled and unhappy. They wanted brains, courage, and heart. Dorothy wanted the power to go home. They were so sure that the key to their desires could be found when they met a wizard in the Land of Oz, so they set out on a lengthy journey down the yellow-brick road to find the things they lacked.

When they got to the end of the road, we all know what happened. They met the wizard and he was a fake. He was a little old man standing behind a curtain. All the little man behind the curtain was able to do was give them symbols of what they wanted — a diploma, a ticking heart necklace, and a badge of courage. Dorothy learned she could click her heels together and get back home. The wizard didn't give them anything they didn't already possess. Everything they pursued to have a fulfilling life was already inside them. They just hadn't used their resources to conquer their circumstances. When we are miserable and full of complaint and pessimism after a Lifeblow, we haven't either. We've left a magnificent gift from God unopened, while we search and wish and hope that we'll find happiness and fulfillment outside of ourselves in a new set of circumstances.

We need not look for a wizard to give us fulfillment in life. All we need to do is use God's gift of choice to give up our reactive humanness and allow God to work in us to reach our God-given potential. With regard to Lifeblows and challenges, we've all heard the statement, "God never gives us more than we can handle." I usually hear that statement as encouraging words for people who are trying to deal with major Lifeblows. The reason I don't care for that statement, is that it's saying that God gave us the Lifeblow. God isn't doling out Lifeblows. The only thing God is doling out is love and guidance to rise above them.

With regard to the idea that everything happens for a reason, I do not disagree. My relationship with God has taught me that the purpose of our life is to use our gift of choice to consciously live in ONENESS with God. Everything in life, good stuff, bad stuff, happens for *that* reason. We've all been blessed with a daily opportunity to hold God's hand, experience God's presence, and be strengthened by God's love.

We do that by inviting God to work in our lives — to open us up to choose new perspectives and receive the outpouring of love, support, and care available from God working through others. In the midst of troubled times, nothing is too much for us to handle when we receive love and return to love with a simple little prayer from our heart, "Guide me."

CHOOSE GOD BY FORGIVING:

"To err is human, to forgive, divine." – Alexander Pope

Two monks were walking on a path through the woods. One was older and the mentor of the other. The walk was very enjoyable and peaceful and serene. After walking for about an hour, the path they were on came to an end. In front of them was a river. They walked to the edge and noticed a woman sitting on a rock. She had been there a while, waiting for someone to come along and help her across. The water was too deep for her, so the older monk picked up the woman and carried her to the other side. Upon reaching the other bank, the woman continued on her way, while the two monks sat down a while to rest.

As they sat and after resuming their walk, the younger monk was visibly upset about something. He kept looking down, obviously consumed with thoughts that were causing him worry and upset. Meanwhile, the older monk walked along smiling, looking up at the towering treetops, feeling the breeze on his face, obviously thoroughly enjoying and appreciating his walk in nature with God. He was living totally in the moment and completely at peace with the world and himself in it. Eventually, the younger monk's worried and unsettled way of being, became so obvious to the older monk, that he stopped walking and asked his friend what was wrong.

The younger monk said that he couldn't stop thinking about what had happened back at the river. He said that everything he had learned as a monk, stated that he should not touch a woman. Yet, he had just observed his mentor, not only touch, but hold and carry a woman when they crossed the river! On hearing the concern in the younger monk's voice, the older looked at him and quietly said, "My dear young brother, you have such heavy thoughts. I set her down on the other side of the river, hours ago. Why in the world are you still carrying her?"

After a Lifeblow, we are often like the younger monk in the above story, told by Heather Forest in *Wisdom Tales from Around the World*. When we carry reactive thoughts about our Lifeblow and get weighed down with worry, disgust, anger, fear, or resentment, our burden doesn't give us an experience of peace. Since many Lifeblows generate feelings of resentment, "Getting Up When Life Blows You Down" requires the realization that when we do carry resentment, we take energy away from our now moment and aren't able to experience God's presence and the fulfillment that comes when we walk with God. When we are feeling anger, hatred, and resentment toward another person, our only option for breaking free and experiencing peace is through our choice to forgive other human beings. When we do that, our lives become transformed for the better in a miraculous way.

Since God IS love, where love is, God is. When we dwell in love, we dwell in God. One way to walk with God, is expressing unconditional love and acceptance for other human beings. Unconditional love is loving without condition, to be loving in spite of conditions, including conditions where another person's words and/or actions have hurt us. Without question, this is one of the most difficult things we will ever do. However, if we want to walk more closely with God, if we want to experience fulfillment, we must learn how to love this way. We must learn how to forgive.

One of the greatest gifts of being shot was that the experience helped me learn about the life transforming power of forgiveness. While asking God for guidance, the message I got about making different choices included choosing a new attitude toward the robber. As you know, my outgoing energy toward him was of hatred and resentment, expressed by visualizing myself beating him with a bat. Shifting that energy would mean shifting my attitude and feelings toward the robber. Since God is love, the shift would have to be away from anger and hatred, to love, through forgiveness.

Had my reactive thoughts about forgiving the robber, been heard out loud, they would have had an incredulous tone. *"Forgive him? Him? The robber? That's completely UNREASONABLE! He violated my freedom. Not only did he take some of my money, he has taken part of my life. He needs to pay for what he has done."* As I continued getting messages from God to forgive the robber, my defensiveness grew into an argument with God about why I was justified and right about being unfor-giving. *"If I forgive him, I'll be doing him a favor. If I forgive him, then basically what I'm saying is that what he did to me is okay . If I forgive him, I'm basically condoning his behavior and giving people permission to treat me poorly. I might as well just let people walk all over me. What am I supposed to do, be walked all over like a rug and pretend that it is no big deal?"*

Every time I thought about forgiveness in that context, I felt like I was disrespecting myself and my reactive thoughts would continue, *"Forget forgiving. It will be a cold day in a very hot place when I forgive the guy who did this."* If my conversations about forgiveness ring a bell to you, it's no wonder we have such a hard time forgiving people who we see as the cause of our Lifeblow! Forgiving another person seems insane when the act of forgiving represents a way to inflict even more pain on ourselves.

Although I struggled a great deal with the idea of forgiving the robber, I knew in my heart that doing so was a directed step from God toward more fulfillment after being shot. In time, I opened up to this idea of forgiving the robber. I wanted to do it, but didn't know how to do it. I related to what Thomas Kempis said, "Be not angry that you cannot make others as you wish them to be, since you cannot make yourself as you wish to be." That quote speaks volumes about our humanness, and I find easy to apply to the act of forgiving. My first breakthrough in my ability to forgive, came as I developed the new perspectives ("new conversations") contained in this book. What dawned on me is that the same principle could be applied to the act of forgiveness.

Remember I said THE QUALITY OF OUR LIFE EXPERIENCE HAS EVERYTHING TO DO WITH THE CONVERSATION WE ARE HAVING ABOUT OUR LIFE EXPERIENCE? This holds true for our experience of forgiving another person. If our perception of forgive-ness is going to change, our conversation about forgiving must change. We must adopt "new conversations" and develop new truths that make the act of forgiving a much easier thing to do. What follows are some "new conversations" and thoughts I adopted, that made it easier for me to forgive the robber who shot me. Perhaps they will be helpful in your forgiveness process as you continue creating fulfill-ment after your Lifeblow.

FORGIVENESS CONVERSATION #1:

"FORGIVING ANOTHER, BEGINS WITH FORGIVING MYSELF."

Since forgiveness is the ultimate expression of LOVE, doing it means giving love away. We've already talked about our inability to give away something we don't already possess. Earlier, I used the metaphor that our body is like a pitcher that can be filled with anything. It can be filled with spring water or it can be filled with acid. The pitcher will hold either one, but if it is full of acid, we can't pour a cool, refreshing glass of water. Even a tiny bit of acid will contaminate the water. Just as we can fill a pitcher with water or acid, we can fill ourselves with love or hate. If we are full of anger, hatred, and resentment, our loving spirit is contaminated and we aren't able to pour out our love. We ultimately choose what we can pour out, by what we choose to keep inside.

During my time in the hospital, I didn't have much love in my heart. Instead, I had hatred, hatred for the robber and what he had done to me. Since love cannot exist in the same space as hatred and resentment, I shared love with no one. I had no love to give away to people who visited me. That's why I turned friends away and had nothing to say to my parents when they initially visited me in the hospital. My outpouring of resentment didn't allow me to give or receive the love that I needed to be uplifted after my Lifeblow.

When we talk about creating and filling our inner environment with love, a natural place to start is with forgiving ourselves. Many people will never find the pathway to forgive anyone for anything because they haven't yet forgiven themselves. That was my barrier to forgiveness when I was in the hospital. Not only was I beating the robber in my mind, I was also beating myself up about being at the ATM very early in the morning when I already had money in my wallet. This anger toward myself was as damaging as my anger toward the robber.

If we can't even unconditionally love and forgive ourselves, there's no way we can unconditionally love and forgive another person. That's another reason that chapter 10, *Give Yourself Credit for Being Valuable* is so important. If we don't stop beating ourselves up and forgive and love ourselves for past actions and mistakes, we'll never be able to give our love away by forgiving other people and be uplifted after our Lifeblow.

FORGIVENESS CONVERSATION #2

"THE MORE I SEE MYSELF AS SEPARATE AND DIFFERENT, THE HARDER IT IS TO FORGIVE."

This morning I'm sitting in a coffee shop, one of my favorite places to write. I'm about to get underway with writing and just caught myself doing the exact thing I wanted to write about this morning, which I am about to encourage you NOT to do if you are trying to forgive someone. I'm catching myself holding a big time judgmental attitude toward a lady behind me.

She walked in about ten minutes ago. She is extremely loud and her accent is a bit irritating. She has been talking non-stop ever since ordering her coffee. She's asked every employee in the place, where they are from, to see if any of them agree with her complaint about the weather we're having this time of year. Now she's doting over an infant behind me whose name she just found out is Grover. She's giving her opinion of the name Grover. She likes it and now she's asking the baby's father how old he is and if he has other children. He answers that he is forty and does have other children. Now the lady wants to know their ages. I just glanced back and she is tickling the baby, but the baby doesn't think it's funny. He, like me, looks horrified.

I'm catching myself thinking:

> *"Good grief, doesn't she ever shut up? Oh great, the kid is starting to cry. I can't write in this environment. I think I'll leave and go somewhere else. But this is one of my favorite places — maybe I'll wait. She may leave in a minute. Thank God I don't have to live or work with that woman. Something's got to happen soon. If I stay here much longer, I may be crying like Grover."*

In our day-in and day-out living, we don't naturally see ourselves as being like all other human beings. Instead, our automatic tendency is to highlight our differences with people. We see ourselves as different from other people in every way imaginable, from our physical size and shape, to our age and the color of our skin. We are very aware of and sometimes even declare our differences in our political affiliations, nationality, and where we live geographically. We distinguish between the size of our homes, the size of our bodies, and the size of our wallets. We find differences in the neighborhoods we live in, our careers, professions, income level, attire, and material possessions. We separate ourselves by class, gender, religion, denomination, style of worship, and marital status. We differ in our beliefs about everything from how to raise children to the proper way to conduct oneself in a coffee shop.

As we notice all the ways we are different, we simultaneously judge one another constantly and continuously. We make subconscious decisions about accepting or rejecting people based on our different beliefs about "the way things are supposed to be". In fact, we do that so much, that we actually have a word describing what it is like to meet someone, who apparently has more similarities with us than differences. When we meet someone with similar opinions, beliefs, and styles, we have rapport. When we meet/encounter someone who is not like us because they have a different style or an opposing view or opinion, we have a lack of rapport and we think and feel very differently. We might avoid further interaction or limit our association with them. People can get on our nerves so much that we do what I did in the coffee shop — we evacuate the area.

Since we so naturally position ourselves as different and separate from other people, the gap widens quickly when someone says or does something hurtful and upsetting to us. It's hard enough to unconditionally love ourselves sometimes, much less someone who is very different, and much, much less, when the someone who is different, has hurt us in some way. Forgiveness requires that we close the gap called how we are different and drop the labels we use to separate ourselves from "those other kinds of people."

By no means am I suggesting that we should not celebrate diversity in one another, nothing like that at all. We are each a unique masterpiece and child of God. Never before has there been another human being quite like you and never again will there be. I believe we should appreciate our ancestry, culture, and various talents and interests. I believe we should even work to preserve many of the things that make us different. It would be a very boring world if we were all just alike. That's called cloning. Given the choice to live like sheep or celebrate diversity, I'll pick the later every time.

My point is simply that the forgiving process gets harder as the gap gets widened with a focus on all the ways we are different. Conversely, forgiveness becomes easier when we focus on our similarities as human beings. A good way to focus on our similarities as human beings, is to temporarily suspend our truth that we are different. We can recognize our diversity as something to celebrate, while always honoring one another as children of God – beings of love who at one time as very young children, related to one another solely in that way. We learned the language of "diverse and different" as we grew older, but before that happened, the language of Love is all we knew and all that was in how we related to one another.

Before we learned about diversity, we had no way of defining ourselves as different in the world. When we learned the language of diversity, we began building an identity rooted in how we are different from other people. Said another way, without you I lose part of my identity. You give me my identity by virtue of how I identify you as different.

For example, I am a man because some humans are women. I am tall because some people are short. I don't have an earring because some people do. I have short hair because others have long hair. I am white because some people are of color. I am old because many humans are young. I live in the city because some people say they live in the country. I am a southerner because some people are northerners and others are mid-westerners. I have been to college because other people have not. I don't have a graduate degree because many people do. I am an American because other people are Europeans. I am an Irish American because some people are African Americans. I like country music because many people like jazz. All of these different labels, cover up the undeniable fact that underneath it all, we are the exact same children of God and beings of Love.

In fact, our identities would slowly disappear without one another and how we see ourselves as different. If there were no one on earth shorter than me, I'd lose my identity as someone who is tall.

Expanding on that, if someone who is different from me was removed from the earth every ten seconds, every ten seconds one of the ways I define myself would be gone. Eventually I wouldn't be able to identify myself in any way other than to say I'm human. A self-image stripped of all our labels and definitions of how we are different, is like returning home – to our true self – where there is only unconditional Love and not a single judgmental bone in our body.

When we see ourselves as human beings, adding <u>nothing</u> more than that, our identity is as a child of God – not as a conditioned human who is different from everyone on the planet. Pure Love, without condition; unconditional love; that is the one and <u>only</u> way that it is possible to forgive another person.

We are all alike as members of the human race. The terrorist attacks reminded most of us of that. It is unfortunate that it sometimes takes disaster and death to help us in this way. Think about all the cell phone calls placed by victims of the terrorist attacks, to members of their families. The end of their lives was close at hand, and many of them knew it. As we listened to actual recordings or reports by their family members about what was said, we realized that the same words would have come out of our mouths had we been there. We related to the words "I love you," as what we would say to our loved ones, whether we were placing a final call or receiving one.

We related to people's shock, terror, disbelief, anger, loss, and grief. We shared their feelings and became so understanding from that perspective that we cried with them. We hurt for them. We mourned for them. We comforted them. We searched for them. We gave of ourselves to them. We did all those things because we saw ourselves in them.

Before the attacks, we had great reasons for why we were so different from one another. We distinguished between being a northerner, southerner, and mid-westerner. We distinguished between wealthy and poor, black and white, Christian and Jew, white collar and blue collar, child and adult, and male and female. Policemen and firemen were even differentiated, but after the attacks, all the above distinctions were gone. By the end of the day of terror, there was no Upper Manhattan versus Lower Manhattan. No distinctions were being made between the cities of New York and Washington, DC. No distinctions were made highlighting any differences in gender, height, hair length, skin color, age, income, level of education, geographic home, or political affiliation. The only distinctions that were going on while America was under attack, were that human beings were dead, lost, dying, hurting, and helping.

As people walked out of the dust cloud at Ground Zero, covered in ash, we became the same color. As janitors comforted CEO's, we became the same class. As school kids cried next to senior citizens, we became the same generation. As Christians, Jews, and Muslims prayed together, we became the same faith. As people of every nation, expressed their sorrow and encouragement, we spoke the same language. As we stood in lines and gave our blood, we became the same body. As we watched TV and tears accompanied the lump in our throat, we became the same family. As candlelight vigils were held around the globe, we became the same people. Unity resulted because we erased the lines that defined us as "separate" and "different." Our focus on our differences got lost in our Love. Being lost in Love; that truly is the only space from which the act of forgiving is possible.

FORGIVENESS CONVERSATION #3

"WHEN I SEE ME IN YOU, IT'S EASIER TO FORGIVE YOU."

The key to forgiveness lies in stopping our negative reactions by shifting our focus away from how we are separate and different. When we do that, we open the possibility to be more understanding. Being more understanding comes from the ability to put ourselves in another person's shoes. If we do that, and can see ourselves in other people, we focus on what it is that we share with them and the forgiving process becomes much easier.

So what do we share with someone who has hurt us? — our humanness! Since we share our humanness, and forgiveness is made possible with better understanding, the best area to gain better understanding is with regard to our humanness and why we do what we do. Since we are all human beings, the easiest place to start that process is to take time to better know and understand ourselves. If we do that, all the understanding we gain can be applied to other people.

The better we know ourselves, the easier it is to see ourselves in other people. The easier it is to see ourselves in other people, the more understanding we can be. The more understanding we are, the less we judge one another. The less we judge one another, the more we accept one another. The more we accept one another, the easier it is to forgive people who have wronged us. The better we know ourselves as a human being, the easier it is to forgive.

On the other hand, the less we know ourselves, the less we can see ourselves in others and the more different and separate we perceive ourselves to be. When that is the case, it's easier to be judgmental and make others wrong. That leads to resentment and anger, and moves us further from God and the ability to forgive. Therefore, if forgiving is extremely difficult, yet we want to experience its life-changing power, we must get to know ourselves better.

Understanding other people requires that we understand or somehow relate to where they are coming from or what they are experiencing or going through. Although it is helpful, it's not critical that we have had someone's same experiences to be understanding or relate to them. We can also relate in other ways.

One way is through our feelings. The reason is because we all have them and we all have the same ones. All of us know what it is like to feel sad, hurt, upset, discouraged, disappointed, afraid, violated, angry, happy, frustrated, overwhelmed, etc. Anytime we can see ourselves in other people by relating to their feelings, the glaringly obvious differences between us get moved into the background of how we see them. In other words, our focus shifts to how we are alike.

I've had many experiences where I was reminded of how quickly the feelings we share as human beings can close the we-are-different gap and create relatedness where there apparently isn't any. One occasion was during a five-day seminar that I attended. There were about forty people attending and one of the other attendees was a homosexual man. For the better part of two days, I had been keeping my distance because I had had a bad experience one time when a gay man approached me. I didn't like what happened and wanted nothing to do with anyone who might do something similar. I simply wasn't comfortable.

My thoughts for the first two days of the program were that he and I were about as different as two people on the planet could be. We were on opposite ends of the spectrum, far, far away from having anything in common. On day three, during a group conversation about fear and how it affects human beings, this guy shared an experience he had had about four months back. He had been walking down the street, minding his own business, when someone jumped out and attacked or "gay bashed" him, as he called it. He had been beaten to a pulp, and was talking about it now as the victim of a hate crime. He shared how he was afraid to walk down a dark street by himself, afraid that someone may be waiting in the dark to hurt him again.

As I sat and listened to this guy talk, I realized that I felt the same way about walking down a dark street by myself, not from any experience of a hate crime, but from my experience at the ATM. I related to every word he was saying and, in the snap of a finger, my entire attitude toward him changed. My entire conversation about him changed from *"He's someone I need to stay away from"* to *"He's probably the only person in this room who can relate to how I feel."* I immediately saw myself in this guy and my judgmental attitude toward him vanished.

We later talked about our similar experiences, and he told me of all the people in the room, he figured I would probably be the last person who could relate to his situation. We both got a kick out of that. It's amazing what we might learn and the similarities we might see with other very different people, if we would just get our judgmental selves out of the way.

Whether we remember our past experiences that generated similar emotions or project ourselves into someone's experience and imagine how we might feel the same if we were in their shoes, when we can relate to people through shared feelings, we feel connected to them as fellow human beings.

Another way to use our shared feelings as a way to relate to one another is to remind ourselves that all actions people take, including those that are hurtful, are taken because someone was feeling a certain way. Our feelings are what lead to reactive behavior, some of which is hurtful. We've covered how we are conditioned from childhood to do whatever we do as human beings. I wrote about how our experiences generate a thought process and how repeated thoughts turn into our belief system, which includes beliefs about ourselves, other people, and the world we live in. Those beliefs then determine how we *feel* about certain things, people, and situations, which ultimately impacts our actions. Every human being on the planet earth operates in that manner.

Therefore, we can also find common ground in the conditioning process we share as human beings. My attitude and actions of initially avoiding the homosexual man in that seminar, was a result of my conditioning. My past experience of being approached by a homosexual man created reactive thoughts years later. When I saw the guy in the seminar, it triggered my conditioned beliefs about people like him — "They may be attracted to me and approach me and create a situation that is uncomfortable and really ticks me off." That belief is what gave me the uncomfortable feeling and my uncomfortable feeling is what led to my actions of avoidance. Had my past experience left me with feelings of hatred, and my ignorance led me to hate all homosexuals, my actions might not have been of avoidance. They may have been violent instead. Regardless of where we are in our level of awareness about ourselves, all automatic human actions are a result of feelings that arise because of how we have been conditioned.

When we understand that, I mean really get it because we see it so clearly in ourselves, it becomes easy to see that our actions, even errors and mistakes, are the result of being the best reactive human we could be. Obviously, we all have room for growth, but at any given time, with our current level of awareness and the way we've been conditioned, we are doing our best. Since none of us can do any more than our best, we can forgive ourselves for being human.

Once we do that for ourselves, we can easily apply that wisdom to ALL human beings. The people who hurt us are also human and are doing what they do because of the beliefs and feelings they have developed from their conditioning. This holds true for the moment in which they said or did the something that hurt us. To be forgiving, we don't have to understand someone's actions. We simply have to understand that their actions, although not the *same* as ours, are *like* our actions in the way they result from conditioning by past experiences. We don't have to relate to what they did. We can relate to the mechanism that has all of us do whatever we do.

Consider Osama bin Laden. I absolutely cannot even begin to relate to this guy. I don't have any understanding, based on my own experience, beliefs, and feelings, how anyone could plan and be behind terrorist attacks. I find what happened to be an atrocity. From my perspective, what happened was cold-blooded murder of innocent people.

Although I have no understanding for any of the terrorists' actions, because I don't share any of their beliefs, I do have an understanding of their actions based on what I know about conditioning. Bin Laden's belief about September 11 was that he was getting back at the United States for innocent lives that were lost during past conflicts that the US was involved in. In his opinion, America murdered innocent people and he believes that it is his duty, directed by God, to inflict the same kind of losses on America. To him, the September 11 attacks, were his way of retaliating for something that happened beforehand.

For most of the other people in the world, the attacks of September 11 were unprovoked, out of the blue, insane acts of ruthless murder. The majority of Americans don't view America's prior involvement in military actions, as acts of ruthless killing and bullying. Most Americans have their opinion about how our government could do better, which may include militarily, but we don't see ourselves as killers and bullies who are deserving of being attacked and killed because we got out of bed to go to work. Regardless of how we see ourselves, the terrorist attacks showed us that there are other people in the world who view us very differently.

Although their opinions and beliefs are different, the way their different beliefs have been conditioned in, is exactly the same. Their "conditioned in" different opinion of the way things ought to be may not be the same as yours and mine. However, in the way they came to exist through conditioning, they are every bit as real to the people holding them. We can view a person from that perspective, without supporting, condoning, submitting to, or agreeing with what they have done.

Although the majority of people disagree with Osama bin Laden's mentality, beliefs, and actions, it's interesting that after the terrorist attacks, some expressions by Americans, show conditioning that holds beliefs that are very similar to his. I heard many Americans say they would like to see the country of Afghanistan blown off the face of the earth. I saw e-mails being passed around, showing a "new" picture of the globe, with a body of water existing where Afghanistan used to be.

Perhaps some people were joking and the joke helped them alleviate their stress and tension. However, many people were not joking. They would have thoroughly enjoyed seeing a big hole in the ground where Afghanistan currently is. Had America and the rest of the free world, reacted that way, millions more innocent people would be dead right now. God was even brought into the equation as a way to justify some of the thinking. One e-mail that was passed around, mentioned that it is God's job to forgive, and our job is to arrange the face-to-face meetings.

No matter how we slice it, while most Americans see themselves as vastly different from Osama bin Laden (particularly those who wanted the country of Afghanistan to be removed from the earth), the reality is that there are some huge similarities as human beings. The conversation and thought process for what was appropriate in dealing with one another was almost identical. The attitude shared by some patriotic Americans and Osama bin Laden was: *"They need to be destroyed. They have killed thousands of innocent people and we need to make them pay by killing them. When we do that, we'll be pleasing God, helping God, and doing God a favor."* Each side wanted to arrange face-to-face meetings, for the other, with God. I suppose if enough people acted on that belief, every day would be like September 11, 2001. It's always easier to relate to people when we see that what we hate most in others, we often deny in ourselves. People who see themselves in one another, generally aren't killing each other.

Regardless of where you stand with your very good conditioned-in opinion of what should or shouldn't be done to make the world a better place, my point here is to simply show how much alike we are as reactive human beings. Whether the people holding the above opinion are loyal Americans who value family and life, or terrorist fighters who don't, when human beings feel attacked and bullied, they want to retaliate the same way.

This entire book is about breaking out of our disaster producing, reactionary humanness. One of my favorite examples of taking the higher road and walking with God is the story of Reginald Denny.

Denny is the truck driver who innocently drove his truck into the middle of rioting that was going on in L.A. in the aftermath of the Rodney King verdict, which acquitted a group of policeman who were caught on video tape, beating King during an arrest. Not knowing what was going on in the area, Reginald Denny was stopped and pulled out of his truck and into the street by an angry mob. A news helicopter flying overhead captured videotape footage of him being beaten and kicked in the head.

One of the rioting men was later identified and arrested. After the riots, Reginald Denny was a guest on the *Oprah Winfrey Show* and was asked what he thought should happen to the guy who was beating him. Denny told the audience that he thought the guy should be let out of jail so he could do community service to help clean up the neighborhood. The entire audience was stunned at his response. How could he say that about someone, who had beaten him so badly?

Denny's response showed his understanding of human beings. He said that the guy who was beating him had never been in trouble before. Emotions were running high about this race issue and the Rodney King verdict. Reginald Denny saw the big picture. He knew the beating was an unchecked reaction that human beings have, no different from the reactions of police officers after high-speed chases and violent resistance. He also knew that we have a long way to go with race relations in this country. Denny saw how a reaction to keep the guy in jail (to get back at him), would not help bring us closer together, but only add fuel to a fire that had been burning out of control. That's why Reginald Denny told the audience, *"It* (racism) *has to end somewhere and it might as well start with me."*

Chinese philosopher, Confucius, said, "Those who cannot forgive others, break the bridge over which they themselves must pass." I think Reginald Denny understood that. I also think that stopping the killing of innocent people will take enough people from every corner of the globe, to adopt the understanding of Reginald Denny. It will take communication and knocking down barriers that are created by attitudes that we are separate and different. It will take people on every side coming together with the realization that God is love; God is not smiling when we kill one another, and God is not applauding at how we have passed the buck about the forgiveness process. Yes, we are all forgiven by God and yes, as Godly creations, created in God's image — it is OUR job to forgive one another.

FORGIVENESS CONVERSATION #4

"WHEN I SEPARATE HUMAN ACTIONS FROM A HUMAN BEING, I CAN FORGIVE MYSELF AND OTHERS FOR BEING HUMAN."

Being understanding by seeing ourselves in another, in how we share our feelings and conditioning, helps us forgive people for being human, just like ourselves. The above conversation furthers that process by helping us see that our resentment and anger is really directed to the result of a person's conditioning, NOT directed to the human being (like ourselves), within whom that conditioning took place.

A powerful exercise for forgiveness is to visualize a beautiful and peaceful place in your mind's eye. Close your eyes and imagine a shady clearing in the woods along a stream. You might prefer visualizing a scene at the beach or on a mountaintop. In any event, visualize this place and put the person you are resenting, into the picture. The key is to see them as the human being they were, <u>before</u> they were conditioned. See them as a baby, sleeping peacefully in the setting, free of any conditioning and representing a loving and accepting human we all entered the world as. See them as a child, who is simply "being," undistinguishable from the baby you used to be and every person used to be.

Next, visualize a box on the ground, sitting about twenty feet from the sleeping baby and imagine that the person's actions are in the box. The box holds all the actions, as well as the conditioning that led to those actions. In other words, the box holds all the energy that caused your damage and hurt. Next, say to yourself, *"I observe without judgment."* Say that several times, retaining the image of the baby — separate from your issue with the conditioned adult version.

When we separate the human being from their conditioning, we can see conditioning as the culprit, not the human who is being. We see that our anger and resentment is directed to human conditioning, instead of toward the specific person we want to forgive. It's easy to stay mad at a living breathing adult jerk who hurt us. By separating the conditioning from the person, it makes it harder to hold onto our anger and resentment, the cause of our unfulfilling life. It is very difficult to be mad and stay mad at a sleeping baby. It's also very difficult to be mad and resentful and stay that way toward a box. Particularly when we see ourselves in the baby, as well as the box.

This is how I was able to forgive the robber. I separated the human ACT of robbing and shooting me, from the HUMAN BEING that I also was. When I did that, I could see that I was hating the act of robbery, not the person who robbed me. When we separate the human act from the human being, we can forgive people for being just like us. We can forgive people for being human.

The robber was very young, fifteen or sixteen years old, and told me during the robbery that he needed the money for crack cocaine. On the surface, I can't think of two people who were more different or anyone who would be harder for me to relate to. We were of a different ethnic background and age, with different habits and different views on appropriate ways to get money. We were already separate and different before 9/28/88, and the chasm got much bigger when he robbed me. With all our differences, forgiveness would require that I put myself in his shoes and somehow see myself in him — to be understanding by relating to his feelings and how our conditioning process is alike.

My encounter with Jeffrey at the shelter for abused and battered women, which I mentioned in chapter 16, helped me see how easily influenced we all were as children. I remember being fifteen or sixteen years old. I remember being easily influenced by older kids. I could see that if I had been the robber and influenced by whomever and whatever he was exposed to, I might have wound up in the same place. Instead of feeling peer pressure to try beer at age fifteen, I might have tried crack cocaine if that was what was being offered to me over and over again.

I am very naïve about drugs, but I did learn from people who knew about crack cocaine that it is very addictive. I was told that if someone slipped me crack cocaine today, I could be addicted tomorrow and be desperate to get more. By imagining myself as desperate for something that my survival depended on, I could see myself doing a lot of things that I wouldn't otherwise do. Had I been in his shoes, I can't honestly say I wouldn't have done the same thing that he did.

During my hospital stay, while talking to one of the detectives investigating the case, he told me that the robber might be just like some of the other people he had dealt with. He may have come to the ATM to rob someone, with no intention of actually shooting someone. He said the robber might be scared to death about what had happened, instead of gloating over it.

When I heard that, I immediately thought of an experience I had when I was thirteen. I was walking with a friend of mine in woods behind my house. We came upon a parked car, which belonged to a man who was fishing in a nearby river. He couldn't see us, so as a prank, we lit an entire pack of firecrackers, threw them into his car, and ran like crazy. After getting a safe distance away, we turned to see if the man had returned to his car. To our horror, flames were shooting out of the driver-side window and the interior of the car was engulfed in flames. This wasn't what we planned! We just wanted to make some noise and disrupt the man's fishing. To try to correct this terrible and unintended result, we ran back toward the car to try to put the fire out, but before we could do anything, the man who had been fishing came running out of the woods. Scared to death, we ran away again. We felt horrible and were terrified that we would go to jail. We didn't mean for anything like that to happen and for years, we never spoke a word of it.

If the robber really didn't intend to shoot someone, I could relate to how he might be feeling. After putting myself in his shoes by thinking of my past experiences, by projecting myself into his experience, and relating to how he might have felt or be feeling, I could see how my humanness and his humanness were really no different. I could hate his actions and the way he had been conditioned and <u>stop</u> hating him as a human being. I could forgive him with my understanding and compassion for a kid who was a lot like me when I was his age.

FORGIVENESS CONVERSATION #5

"FORGIVENESS IS A GIFT WE GIVE OURSELVES."

As I mentioned at the beginning of this segment on forgiveness, one of the things that makes forgiving so difficult, is that we associate it with bowing down to someone who hurt us. We associate it with allowing someone to walk all over us and we think that forgiving means that we should just forget about what happened and go on our merry way. In forgiving someone it seems like we are condoning the actions that hurt us. Breaking out of this very limiting and false interpretation of forgiveness is critical if we want to experience fulfillment.

A great motivator to forgive people who have hurt us, lies in understanding and recognizing the price we pay for not forgiving. In chapter 3 on "Avoiding A Natural Disaster," you identified how you win and how you lose with your reaction to your challenge. You got clear on what kind of life you created while you were experiencing hatred, anger, frustration, discouragement, etc. and leaving your expression of those emotions unchecked. When you remind yourself of the kind of life you create while harboring resentment, you are able to see how your reactions take you further from the kind of life you want.

Take a moment to dive into a state of resentment right now. Visualize someone you resent and remember why you feel resentful toward them. Keep talking about how much you hate them and what you want to do to them and keep doing to get back at them. Do that for ten minutes or so. Go ahead. Put this book down and dive into resentful humanness. If you did that you've begun to get a sense of how your resentment steals your life.

Notice the blow to your relationships and how it affects your ability to love, trust, be loved, care deeply, and be vulnerable. Notice how you lose your well-being and health. Notice your anxiety and blood pressure rising. Consider the long-term losses from this physical state you are in — losing friends and loved ones, perhaps aging eight years in the next three — maybe having a heart attack or being struck down by a stroke. Notice how unproductive and unsettled you are. Notice the loss of your spirituality and experience of peace. Notice the collective negative impact of holding on to your resentment!

E. B. White said, "One of the most time consuming things is to have an enemy." Few things are more damaging to a life that can be fulfilling, than an unproductive harboring of resentment and hatred toward another human being. After generating such a state of resentment, you can see how your resentment, not your Lifeblow, steals your time and energy and keeps you from a fulfilling life. Garrison Keillor said, "That's what happens when you are angry with people. You make them part of your life." Your Lifeblow is in the past. Your resentment is in the present, and it's like a disease. It fills you with DIS-EASE and will eat you up inside to the degree that you experience no fulfillment, no peace, no joy. We will do ourselves in by not being loving.

That's what my resentment did to me in the hospital. I continued making the robber a part of my life and did myself in. Every morning I woke up, I had my routine, which included, give myself a sponge bath, eat breakfast, read the paper, watch TV, listen to music, and visualize a brutal scene in the woods with a baseball bat. For the remainder of each day, I alternated between watching TV, reading, listening to music, and being a star in my own movie called "Revenge." Visualizing "Revenge" was a routine I repeated four to five times a day. I was a miserable human being, filled with dis-ease, unable to experience any fulfillment.

Once I shifted out of hatred and resentment, and into compassion for the robber, by separating his human being from his human behavior, and saw myself in him, my shift in feelings created a shift in energy. My hate energy spent visualizing myself beating him got redirected with an entirely new focus.

Here's how: The day after becoming more compassionate and understanding of the robber, I woke up in the same physical environment. I was confined to the same bed, surrounded by the same four walls of the same hospital room, on the same hallway, on the same floor, of the same hospital, on the same street, of the same block, in the same city, and surrounded by all the same people. The morning after forgiving the robber, I began my normal routine again. Starting with a sponge bath, it eventually became time to watch myself star in the movie "Revenge" again, and bring some good old hateful feelings to life.

When I closed my eyes to begin my internal reign of terror, I couldn't do it. I was unable to follow through as a bat-wielding maniac. Since my current energy was flowing out of understanding and compassion, beating someone with a bat was no longer an option. Hatred beats people with a bat, but compassion does not, so beating the robber was no longer something I had any interest in doing. Therefore, if I wasn't going to do that, I wanted to find something else to do. I wanted to find something else to occupy my time.

In the "looking for" something else to do, I was living with a new focus. Looking around the hospital room became a brand new experience. I was looking through new lenses and saw a new world in my hospital room. Perhaps the most profound thing that happened is that for the first time in two months, I really NOTICED the four walls in my hospital room. I had been looking at them for over two months, but my anger and resentment prevented me from really "seeing" them and appreciating what they represented. The walls were covered with cards and banners that people had sent to wish me well and to have a speedy recovery.

In addition to the cards, two tables in the room and the windowsill were covered with plants and flowers people had sent to brighten my days. Before now, my room had represented a prison cell that everyone was calling a hospital room. After forgiving the robber, my hospital room represented a space that oozed love and caring from my friends and family, through the cards and flowers that were there. After noticing the love, my attitude instantly shifted dramatically toward that of gratitude for the people in my life, as I mentioned in chapter 12, "Adopt an Attitude of Gratitude." I felt loved and cared for and began welcoming my friends and cherishing the opportunity to visit with them and my family. With that change, I regained my experience of what it is like to love and be loved. I experienced God's presence. I experienced the peace that comes with knowing we are not alone in our struggle.

Forgiving the robber, opened the door to feeling gratitude for the people in my life, which led to feelings of gratitude for just being alive and having another day to live on this earth. It helped me notice that some people in the hospital were less fortunate. As you already know, that awareness led to our giving plants and flowers to other patients and experiencing the rewards of God's love returning in the form of their company and smiles.

Forgiveness truly was a gift for myself. Once we begin the forgiveness process, the physical world remains while our experience of it is transformed. We gain new life when our focus and energy is redirected from hatred and resentment TO love and compassion for others AND gratitude for our gifts and blessings. Once we experience the rewards of forgiveness, the act becomes an easier and sought after alternative in the future when we've been hurt by another in a big or small way. Marie Stopes said, "You can take no credit for beauty at sixteen. But if you're beautiful at sixty, it will be your soul's own doing." I relate her words to forgiveness.

Had I never learned how to forgive, with all the opportunities to do so with other people since being shot, I know my baggage would be heavy. I also know that the quality of my life while lugging it around would fall somewhere between reasonably unhappy and miserable. My life would be ugly. My Lifeblow at the ATM helped me learn that forgiveness doesn't mean to forget. Forgiveness means to remember with peace. I have never forgotten anything that has happened to me, particularly where I've been left feeling very angry and hurt. I've simply remembered with peace. Forgiveness makes that possible and provides a source of profound transformation and fulfillment.

Remembering with peace gives me hope that the robber is doing seminars somewhere today on "How To Turn Your Life Around"; in fact, my fantasy is that one day we are working together, doing a seminar *with* one another and sharing a message about being our best in this life.

So, to the person I met on September 28, 1988, at the Fleet Bank ATM on the corner of Park Avenue and Berkely Street, across from the Big Apple Café in Rochester, NY — if you happen to be reading this, wherever you are, I would enjoy hearing from you. Perhaps we can start anew and meet on new ground. If I never get the chance to tell you in person, please know that I have forgiven. Thanks for being a part of my life. It's one thing to have peace and joy when all is well. It's another, very profoundly different thing, to have peace and joy when the bottom falls out. Without our time together, and what you helped teach me about the act of forgiveness, I may have never learned how to forgive anyone else for anything since then, and that would be my loss.

FINAL THOUGHTS

A big tough samurai warrior once went to see a little monk. "Monk," he said, in a voice accustomed to instant obedience, "teach me about heaven and hell!"

The monk looked up at this mighty warrior and replied with utter disdain, "Teach you about heaven and hell? I couldn't teach you about anything. You're dirty. You smell. Your blade is rusty. You're a disgrace, an embarrassment to the samurai class. Get out of my sight. I can't stand you." The samurai was furious. He shook, got all red in the face, and was speechless with rage. He pulled out his sword and raised it above him, preparing to slay the monk.

"That's hell," said the monk softly. The samurai was overwhelmed. The compassion and surrender of this little man who had offered his life to give this teaching to show him hell! He slowly put down his sword, filled with gratitude, and suddenly peaceful. "And that's heaven," said the monk softly.

After reading the above story in a book called *How Can I Help*, by Rom Dass and Paul Gorman, I immediately thought about how much we are like the samurai warrior in the aftermath of our Lifeblow. We are upset and angry and full of inner turmoil and turbulence. Our anger, worry, anxiousness, restlessness, distrust, hate, resentment, impatience, fear, doubt, and discouragement, give us an experience of life that we describe as going through hell. If that's where we are left after a Lifeblow, it's not where we must stay.

Many people use the saying, "This is a slice of heaven on earth" to describe a beautiful place, experience, or time when they feel peace and fulfillment because they are present to what God has created and made possible. Describing life that way is not normally what we do on a day-to-day basis. It seems as if there are a limited number of occasions during the course of our life where we describe life as "heavenly." Watching your child being born, standing on the rim of the Grand Canyon, and being reunited with family after a lengthy separation, aren't regular occurrences for most of us. However, that doesn't mean we cannot experience life as a slice of heaven on earth on a day-in and day-out basis. We can have life occur that way as often as we choose.

The key is being present to what God has created and made possible — day-in and day-out. Since God is love and created us in His image with the ability to choose, when we consciously choose ways of being that encompass love (patience, kindness, acceptance, gentleness, forgiveness), we walk with God. Said another way, we walk with God when we live our life in a way that love is evident in how we treat other people, express ourselves, and go about our business. When we live that way, God is working through us and reaches the people around us — giving us results and a "now" moment experience that we might describe as heavenly. The reason is because we are experiencing something God has created and made possible.

Each "new conversation" gives us access to that kind of experience because it represents an opportunity to live our lives as God intended; that is, using our God-given resources to rise above our circumstances. Each new perspective is a gateway to fulfillment because it enables us to walk in God's ways instead of our own. Consider the two columns on the opposite page, two fundamentally different ways of being, from which we can choose to live our life.

As you can see, when our reactive ways are running rampant, we are separated from God. In our misery, we may even wonder where God is and why God isn't helping us. We fail to realize that God isn't missing from our life. Our reactive ways have us miss God's presence. Our reaction gives us no chance of experiencing the peace and fulfillment we get when we consciously walk with God. Heavenly experiences aren't possible when immersed in the human reactive way. As you saw in the story about the samurai warrior, how much we experience God depends on how much we get our reactive selves out of the way. When we respond with "new conversations" that enable us to walk in God's ways, we get what God gives away: a transformed

God's Way	The Human Reactive Way
Loving	Hateful
Accepting	Judgmental
Grateful	Ungrateful
Peaceful	Worried and Anxious
Faithful	Fearful and Doubtful
Trusting	Distrustful
Forgiving	Resentful and Angry
Hopeful	Full of Despair
Joyful	Miserable & Distraught
Helpful and Caring	Uncaring
Generous and Giving	Selfish
Compassionate	Indifferent
Kind	Unkind
Patient	Impatient
Understanding	Making others "wrong"
Humble	Boastful/Cocky/Full of Pride
Authentic/Sincere	Inauthentic/Fake

life of peace, joy, and fulfillment. Go back to page 31 and take a look at the column "How I Lose." Notice how all the results in that column get produced by living in "The Human Reactive Way." When we choose "new conversations" that bring us back to "God's Way," we reverse our losses. We turn the tide. We rise to new life. We find fulfillment and peace after our Lifeblow because we come into harmony with God.

A few years ago, I attended a Carolina Panthers football game with some friends. I had been looking forward to this particular afternoon for a long time. It was a beautiful day to be outside watching football and I've always cherished my time with friends. At one point during the game, I had to go to the bathroom. When I got there, all the urinals and toilets were taken, so I stood patiently waiting for one to become available. As I was standing there, another man walked up beside me and asked me which stall I was waiting for. I turned and told him I was waiting for the next available one. He immediately said, "No, you have to pick one!"

In that instant, my human-reaction switch flipped over and I immediately got an attitude. Who did this guy think he was? Now, with a slightly different tone, I repeated myself, "Look, I don't have to pick which one I'm going to use. I'm waiting for the next available toilet." Once again, he informed me that I had to choose the one I wanted to use. An argument ensued about how lines in men's bathrooms work. Our voices got louder and neither one of us was doing a very good job of winning the other over to our opinion of the way things are supposed to be.

The next words about to come out of my mouth were, "Here's the deal: One of these stalls is going to open up in a few seconds, hopefully, and when it does, it's got my name all over it. If you have anything else to say about it, we'll just have to throw down right here and solve it that way." As those words reached the tip of my tongue, I noticed my natural human reaction and the disaster I was about to create. Standing there in the bathroom, what flashed across my mind, was a vision of me rolling around and fighting on the bathroom floor, being arrested and led out of the stadium, and feeling horrible and embarrassed as people looked at me and whispered to one another, "Look. There goes that motivational speaker." I saw myself going to jail, having to post bail, missing the game, missing an afternoon with friends, and probably ruining their afternoon spent getting me out of my predicament.

When I saw where I was about to go with my reaction, it occurred to me that I hadn't awakened that morning and jumped out of bed, excited about fighting at the Panthers game and being kicked out; however, I was about to go there — over a toilet! As soon as I saw what I was doing, I stopped reacting. I refocused on a vision of what I wanted — being with friends and having a fun afternoon. I shifted to an attitude of gratitude for the chance to spend my time that way. I accepted responsibility for what I was about to create and my "why" was big enough to practice self-control. I remembered I am not my feelings of mad, and mad didn't have to be my expression toward the other guy in the bathroom. I could just as easily choose to selflessly give and abundantly receive.

So that's what I did. I stepped back, turned to this other reactive human who had to go to the bathroom and said, "Go ahead."

He looked at me, completely taken off guard, and said "What?" almost as if he wasn't sure if he had heard me correctly.

I repeated myself, "Go ahead." adding "If it's that important to you that you use the bathroom first, then go ahead."

The man looked down as if thinking about what had just happened, and looked back up at me and said, "That's okay. It's cool. You go ahead."

Seconds later, one of the stall doors opened. I walked in, used the bathroom, and returned to my seat. Amazing what using these "new conversations" can generate! I got exactly what I wanted and it didn't happen because I won a fight rolling around on the bathroom floor. It happened because I was walking in God's ways. I simply chose some of the "new conversations" in this book and became a more loving person. In the process, I got a heavenly experience outside on a beautiful day with my friends.

The only way a heavenly experience of life can be realized when consumed by anger during and after a Lifeblow, is through forgetting self and sending love when we become aware of our need to be right about our reactive ways.

We uncover our loving spirit when we get our ego out of the way. This entire book is about operating after a Lifeblow from that unselfish place by stopping our unhealthy reaction and giving up our need to be right about our reactive perceptions. While experiencing a sunset as a "slice of heaven on earth", we aren't self-absorbed in our complaint about life or making the world wrong in that instant. If we were, the setting sun would simply occur as the end of an awful, unfair day. In forgetting self in the same manner after a Lifeblow, we can return to love, walk in God's ways, and experience life as a heavenly experience.

After the terrorist attacks, Timothy Patterson, a minister at the church I attend, spoke of walking in God's ways during one of his sermons. He said, "I was struck by the astonishing contrast between the suicidal hijackers and those courageous passengers on Flight 93 and other heroes — the difference between those who are willing to die to kill others and those who are willing to die to save others. And that's when the words of Jesus from the Gospel of John came to me in the middle of the night with new power and vivid meaning. 'There is no greater love than this, to lay down one's life, to give one's life for one's friends.' That is what many people did during the terrorist attacks; they gave their lives to save others." He proceeded to remind us of inspiring examples of such love.

During the attacks, we saw that pattern of self-giving love over and over again. George Howard, a New York City policeman who had a day off when the terrorists struck, saw the events unfolding on TV and flew out of the house to save the people of his city. He rushed to the World Trade Center and while helping those in need, was killed by falling debris. There is no greater love than this, to lay down one's life to save another's life.

We saw the same selfless giving in many office workers who helped one another down the stairs and to safety, including an older Jewish man who's friend was a paraplegic in a wheelchair. They had worked side-by-side for over twenty years, and when his disabled friend told him to get out, he refused to go. Instead, he helped his friend place a phone call to his wife and then made his own call. After reaching his nephew, who asked why he wasn't trying to escape the burning building, he simply said that he couldn't risk letting his friend die alone. Moments later, they died together when the tower they were in collapsed. Neither one of them died alone. There is no greater love than this, to lay down one's life for one's friends.

Then there's the story of the Reverend Mychal Judge, a Franciscan priest who responded to the call with the firefighters. As the beloved chaplain of the New York City Fire Department, Father Mike responded with the love of God in his heart — to help the firemen get through tragedy, as he had so many times before. While giving Last Rites to one of his fallen firefighters, Father Mike was struck and killed. His body was carried out of the rubble and down the street by a group of firefighters, who gently laid his body at the altar of a nearby church. There is no greater love than this, to give one's life for one's friends.

Every moment of every day, we have the opportunity and privilege to grow in oneness with God, by making choices to shift perspective, forget self, and operate and interact with love. Ty Herndon sings a song that contains lyrics that say it all about the power of love.

> *Tell me something, who could ask for more*
> *Than to be living in a moment*
> *Loving every minute.*
> *Tell me something, who could ask for more*
> *Than to be living in a moment you would die for.*

Only love has the power to create that kind of moment. The kind of moment that is so purposeful and meaningful and selfless - that ego disappears, and with it – all concern about dying. It is only by living in love by walking in God's ways, that we make the absolute most of this life. One way to look at this life is to imagine that you and I are standing on a beach. It is early in the morning and you are holding a huge spool of fishing line. I'm standing in front of you and take the end of that line in my fingers. I begin walking down the beach. As I walk, the line slowly comes off the spool you are holding. I walk and walk, minutes pass, then hours, until finally I disappear from your view.

Although you can't see me, when you look down, the fishing line continues coming off the spool. Late into the night, you wonder when the spool will be empty, but the line keeps coming off. This goes on for a week, night and day, day-in and day-out, until finally all the line has come off the spool. You drop the empty spool and now hold your end of the line. You tie a knot in the fishing line, approximately one inch from the end. You look at the knot and consider how much space it consumes along the entire length of line that is stretched between us.

The entire length of the line between us represents everlasting life. The knot represents this human life, the one I'm living as I write this book and the one you're living as you read it. Comparatively speaking, this is a short life. My Lifeblow happened on one morning of one day in the "knot" that represents all the days of my life as a human being. Viewing life from that perspective helps to see how much significance we sometimes bring to even the smallest issues in our life as humans. This is a new day, not a new knot. In all the days of this very short life, never will there be a better, timelier opportunity to have peace and fulfillment than right now.

Erma Bombeck said, "When I stand before God at the end of my life, I would hope that I would not have a single bit of talent left and could say, 'I used everything you gave me.'" Our ability to choose is a gift from God. Using it to start the "new conversations" in this book and become a new creation and more loving person, is our gift to God. Giving that to God over and over in our daily living, at higher and higher levels, is the supreme work we have in this life.

A cartoon I saw in a newspaper after the terrorist attacks showed firefighters running up the stairs of the World Trade Center, faster and faster, forgetting themselves to find people in need and help their fellow human beings. The cartoon showed firemen standing on clouds at the gates of heaven. They were wearing their rescue uniforms, with halos above their helmets, and reporting into their walkie-talkies, "We've reached the top."

At the end of our lives, I hope God is smiling at how we — like those firefighters — loved so fully and selflessly and reached the top of our God-given potential. Lifeblows provide an awesome opportunity to grow in that direction. Growing in that direction is a choice. It is a guarantee for getting up and thriving when the winds of change howl. When life blows you down, God bless you — as you tie a heavenly knot in your short stay here.

About the Author

Bill Dyer's world was seemingly turned upside down by two life threatening experiences that changed his life forever. While selling commercial explosives to the mining and construction industries in the late 1980s, Bill was robbed and shot at an Automatic Teller Machine on his way to work and, then, he was nearly killed in an explosives blast two years later. Powerful lessons for leading and prospering in challenging times have been gleaned from these experiences; in fact, they inspired Bill to become a professional speaker, author, and coach. For thirteen years, wisdom gained from these challenges has been at the heart of his purpose to help others during difficult times.

Bill's message and programs help people achieve peak performance by making powerful choices and being unstoppable in the face of self-limiting beliefs and attitudes, which grow out of challenges, adversity, growth, and change. Former clients include: Celebrity Cruises, Kirby, The CIA, US Postal Service, Martin Marietta, Jefferson Pilot, Novartis, Wake Forest Graduate School of Management, National Home Furnishings Association, National Homebuilders Association, and Coldwell Banker.

Born in Wichita Falls, Texas, Bill Dyer grew up in Jacksonville, Florida. After graduating from Tulane University in 1983 with a degree in Geology, he worked as a geologist in the oil fields of Kansas, Colorado, Utah, and Wyoming. In 1985, Bill went to work for Western Geophysical on the exploration side of the oil and gas industry, managing offshore exploration crews along the Louisiana-Texas Gulf Coast and West Africa.

Upon returning to the US in 1988, Bill took a position with Dupont, selling commercial explosives, before pursuing his dream of working for himself. In 1991 he started a business distributing alarm systems for a marketing arm of Applied Electronics. For four years, speaking and leading seminars were a vital part of building a national business. Bill's passion for that role led to the creation of his personal development company, Quantum Leap Resources, in 1994.

Bill Dyer's Speaking, Seminar, and Coaching Topics

TOPIC # 1: RISING ABOVE MOUNTAINOUS CHALLENGES

Based on his experiences of being robbed and shot and then almost killed in an explosives blast, Bill shares insights for being your best during difficult times of change.

As a member of his audience, you feel the tension, terror, and anxiety of being robbed at gunpoint. You sense the disbelief and shock after a gunshot breaks the early morning silence and finds its victim. You understand a hopeless outlook when the end is near. While listening to Bill and considering your challenges in life — you begin to see opportunities to grow into your highest potential. You see openings for action to produce extraordinary outcomes.

This topic delivers the maverick mindsets and tools for being a highly effective leader in your life and of your life to achieve your desired results. You are left touched, inspired, and prepared to rise above your challenges and setbacks like a champion.

TOPIC # 2: PROSPERITY MINDSETS FOR WORKING WITH OTHERS

When people of different backgrounds, experiences, and perceptions interact and work together, "disagreements" and conflict are likely to arise — followed by blaming, back-biting, gossiping, aggression, withholding, avoidance, arguing, or silent treatment. Conflict can be disastrous for an organization, community, or family. However, it can also be an opportunity for people to grow closer, create a more friendly environment, get more done, and have more fun. This topic will help you change your paradigms about conflict. Whether with a co-worker, employer, employee, associate, customer, neighbor, friend, or family member, you will learn how to spend less energy creating the relationships you want by stopping futile attempts to change other people. This topic focuses on powerful ways of listening and interacting, to turn conflict around on a dime and create a win/win path forward.

Topic # 3: Reaching Your Highest Potential, It's All In Your Head

Reaching your highest potential is more about being the right person than becoming the right person. In other words, all you need to be your absolute best is already inside you. Accessing your greatness, is simply a matter of removing barriers that block the way to your higher plateau. Barriers present themselves as the lack of a compelling vision, fear, not having motivating and measurable goals, living out of balance, operating under stress, procrastination, and self limiting beliefs. This topic delivers the tools for breaking through these barriers. Once these destroyers of human potential are recognized and removed, you find yourself in a clearing of new and very real possibility for your life. Not "pie in the sky" possibility, but an entirely new reality of what you can accomplish and achieve. You learn the keys to motivating yourself, and others, to reach the mountaintop of desired destinations.

* All programs are tailored to accomplish the specific objectives of each client.

I welcome the opportunity to discuss your event, learn about your objectives, and work with you to create a program that makes a powerful and lasting difference for your people.

– Bill Dyer

Quantum Leap Resources
7660 Smullian Trail West
Jacksonville, FL 32217
Phone: (904) 464-0064
E-mail: atmbdyer@aol.com
Website: www.billdyer.com

What Clients Say About Bill's Programs

"We have had a number of guest speakers from outside our industry, and many quite good, in fact. Your one-hour was far and above any other I have heard. The fact that you were virtually mobbed afterward by our accounts is testimony to your performance."
– Benton Bryan, President
John H. Daniel Company

"We have been having award banquet speakers for many, many years - and I have received more compliments on your presentation than any in the past."
– Stephen Culler, President
Coldwell Banker, Lambe Young Realtors

"I was extremely impressed and delighted by your ability to use the specific changes affecting CP&L. Numerous comments from various N.A. Consumer Sales Team members have indicated the positive impact your program has had since the workshop. We know we will be a more productive contributor to CP&L."
– John Borek, Sales Manager
Carolina Power & Light

"Many phrases used by you were repeated by conference attendees during the week, so I know that your message made a positive impression."
– Mark Wernet, Director
Brad Ragan, Inc.

"You reached each person in our meetings spanning a diverse group of people. We have heard many compliments on your program. The most valued are the ones we see and hear in the positive attitudes and actions of our team. We feel the benefits of your work continue to multiply."
– Kay D. Wall, CEO
Bryant Electric Company, Inc.

"As a meeting planner I know the value of a great speaker. You are a newfound treasure."
– Kay McCoy, Director of Member Services
South Carolina Pharmacy Association

"Thank you for a marvelous program!"
– Melissa Leighton, Director, Executive Officers Council
National Association of Home Builders

"They say the second time is a charm. Most of the post conference surveys rated your presentation as the highlight of our business sessions. I hope we can go for a 'triple' soon."
– Mark Singer, Executive Director
Advocates of VA -Association & Management Services

"Sitting at the head table, my reading of the crowd was confirmed by the large number of comments after the meeting. Believe me — you were an OVERWHELMING hit!"
– Sandy McAdams, Chair
Sales & Marketing Council of NC

QUICK ORDER FORM

Fax Orders: (904) 730-4718 (Send this form or a photocopy.)

Telephone Orders: Call 877-BILL-DYER (877-245-5393)
                  (Have your credit card ready.)

Postal Orders: Quantum Leap Resources
                   Fulfillment
                   7660 Smullian Trail West
                   Jacksonville, FL 32217

PLEASE SEND THE FOLLOWING:

Book: *When Life Blows You Down*   Qty _____ @ $ 15.95 = _____

  SUB TOTAL... _____

  SALES TAX: Please add 6.5% for products
             shipped to Florida addresses......................... _____

  SHIPPING: $3.50 for first product and $ 1.00 for
              each additional book..................................... _____

  TOTAL.. _____

Method of Payment: __ Check or Money Order   __ Credit Card

Type of Card: __ Visa   __ MasterCard   __ AmEx   __ Discover

Card Number: _____

Name on Card: _____ Exp. Date _____

Signature: _____

Ship To:
Name: _____

Address: _____

City: _____ State: _____ Zip: _____

Telephone: _____ E-Mail: _____

I WANT TO HEAR FROM YOU!

Thanks for letting me into your life for this short time.
I'd like to know what you think about
When Life Blows You Down
— your most favorite parts, least favorite parts, and what effect,
if any, this book has had on your life.

Your feedback is important to me and greatly appreciated!

Please send your thoughts to:

When Life Blows You Down
Quantum Leap Resources
7660 Smullian Trail West
Jacksonville, FL 32217